The Son of My Father

The Memoir of a Preaching Minister/Educator

by John W Waters, PhD.

The contents of this work, including, but not limited to, the accuracy of events, people, and places depicted; opinions expressed; permission to use previously published materials included; and any advice given or actions advocated are solely the responsibility of the author, who assumes all liability for said work and indemnifies the publisher against any claims stemming from publication of the work.

All Rights Reserved
Copyright © 2023 by John W Waters, PhD.

No part of this book may be reproduced or transmitted, downloaded, distributed, reverse engineered, or stored in or introduced into any information storage and retrieval system, in any form or by any means, including photocopying and recording, whether electronic or mechanical, now known or hereinafter invented without permission in writing from the publisher.

Dorrance Publishing Co
585 Alpha Drive
Suite 103
Pittsburgh, PA 15238
Visit our website at www.dorrancebookstore.com

ISBN: 979-8-89027-407-6
eISBN: 979-8-89027-905-7

Dedication

To Lili and Robert Ingram, Rachael Moorman, and the many friends and members of The Greater Solid Rock Baptist Church for their support and encouragement over the years. Also to the memory of my dear mother, Mary Annie Randall Waters, who loved me in spite of.... May the blessings of God rest upon each of you. To God be the glory....

Contents

Introduction 7

Chapter One 12
   Education Begins

Chapter Two 21
   Do Not Let That Which You Cannot Do...

Chapter Three 27
   When You Have Done All That You Can...

Chapter Four 33
   When You Have Done All That... (Part 2)

Chapter Five 46
   I Have All that I Need, Except Those Things I Do Not Have...

Chapter Six 49
   The Gift of Memory

Chapter Seven 54
   The Seminary Years

Chapter Eight 67
   Whom God Calls, He Qualifies...

Chapter Nine 74
   You Should Not Judge a Book By...

Chapter Ten 80
   Blessed Assurance

Chapter Eleven 85
   My Faith Looks Up to Thee

Chapter Twelve 88
   The Long Journey

Chapter Thirteen 94
   Putting It All Behind and Moving Forward

Chapter Fourteen 100
   Developing the Church to Move Forward

Chapter Fifteen 108
   Everything Is Subject to Change Except...

Chapter Sixteen.. 113
   Precious Memories How They...

Chapter Seventeen 119
   Living in Appreciation...

Chapter Eighteen 136
   Look Where He's Brought Me From

Introduction

While visiting a church recently, one of its members asked me, "If you could live your life over, would you do anything differently?" The brother who asked the question and I are alumni of the same high school, but not from the same year. He is very much my junior, and I have known him for several years.

His question was not new to me, although it did provide me with a moment to reflect on a long and challenging life that began in Atlanta, Georgia, during the midst of the Great Depression. My response, after only a few seconds, was, "No, there is nothing that I would do differently, but there are several things that I would do three or four times over."

I am an educator, and knew from the age of around three that I wanted to teach. However, I now describe myself as a professional educator rather than a teacher. Doing this allows me to explain to others the difference between being an educator and a teacher. Simply put, an educator seeks to teach people how to think; whereas a teacher focuses on teaching others what to think. One stresses a thought-process, the other indoctrination. My explanation ends in most cases with, "A thinking people is a dangerous people."

An opening statement for a discussion of my life growing up in the South would be a "Colored Grady Baby"—the ninth of ten children, the seventh of eight sons born to Henry and Mary A. Waters. As an infant, my parents were told I had a medical condition that would cause me to die before the age of five. That was more than eighty years ago. Growing up, I was a somewhat sickly child, suffering from the condition for which much later I would have major surgery. As a sickly child, my father and I were often at odds given his other children, especially his sons, were healthy and working and out of his house by their early teenage years. I would be somewhat of an exception.

My formative years occurred during World War II, with six of my seven brothers at one time or another being enlisted in the military. Five of my brothers were in the US Army, and one was in the US Navy. Blackouts, air raids, and various drills were common during my elementary school days until the war ended. Given the numbers of her sons in the military, my mother dreaded getting a letter through the Western Union, but she never did. Over my life, there have been major military conflicts from World War II, Korea, Vietnam, and Iraq. I wish I could declare that the world is safer now than it has been during my lifetime, but such simply is not true. Along with many, my feeling is that we are living through one of the most dangerous and stressful periods of the nation's history.

My mother had the habit of gathering her children and reading to them. With older brothers and sisters, books were always around to be read. Thus, I entered the first grade as an excellent reader. The seed to becoming a teacher may have been planted by my mother, who not only took time to read to me but to teach me how to read. My mother was thirty-eight when I was born.

The focus of my memoir will be things learned about and from life over a career as an educator. This career began around the age of nine by teaching in my Sunday school and Baptist Training Union (BTU, BYTU) because of my reading ability and enthusiasm for learning and sharing with others what I knew. To say the least, sometimes in church, a traditional urban/rural Black Baptist one, questions I asked to a teacher would provoke the response, "The devil made you ask that." Later, it dawned on me that the teacher did not know the Bible that well and simply taught what had been passed on to her. These were committed believers in the church who gave so freely of themselves to help others believe that Jesus came to save us all.

One of the basic affirmations of life that I learned and affirm states simply, "Education begins at birth and ends at death, therefore, as

Introduction

long as there is breath in you, you should be in the process of learning something. One is never too young to learn or too old to learn, but may be too stubborn to learn." This simple principle has led me from an alleyway of Atlanta, where my parents lived when I was born, to the halls of some well-known colleges and universities throughout the free world. This statement is the way each lecture and workshop I give begins. In addition, those listening to me will hear, "Whatever you focus upon will increase." So, a focus on learning assures one that his/her learning will increase.

A second affirmation follows logically from the first: "How do you teach a people who do not wish to be taught?" For an educator, this is a real challenge. So often, there are those sitting in front of the teacher who would seem to have a complete resistance and disregard to learning something new. They seem satisfied with their limited "education" and see no reason to entertain any new thoughts or concepts. Such people are found in almost every socio-economic group. My response first is to say that often it is necessary to "trick" someone into learning something new and/or different. The best approach to this is through the proper motivation. That is, with the proper motivation, learning is possible at almost every mental and physical level. However, you must realize that "change takes place immediately; the decision to change may take time." This affirms also that everything we know had to be learned. A good educator understands this.

A third co-essential to these two affirmations is "Do not let that which you cannot do keep you from doing that which you can do." In other words, do not let history control one's destiny. Too often, there is a focus on what has not been done or accomplished rather than what has. It would seem more appropriate to focus on what can be done rather than what has not been done and the reasons for such, which corresponds to the saying, "to continue to do the same things without any positive results is the definition of insanity." I am told that this is a conclusion Albert Einstein came to following many of his experiments. Yet, there are so many who repeat past errors without ever learning from them. Why would someone keep trying something that does not work? This, too, is a problem that the professional educator must address. There is an expression that states: "those who do not know history are doomed to repeat the same mistakes."

"Do not let that which you cannot do keep you from doing that which you can do." This statement is a corollary of the affirmations from life just given. Somewhere, I heard or read, "We live in crisis, coming out of one and going into another," which suggests that no current condition or situation should hinder one's movement forward. Nowhere or no one of whom I know has ever suggested there is a perfect lifestyle—perhaps a preferred one but not a perfect one. However, it is expected that from one's life there come experiences that help in achieving goals and objectives. Life in its fullest, I came to learn through teaching and trying to educate others, has real meaning when positive steps are taken toward realistic goals that have been predetermined. This valuable lesson I learned as a student of Art Williams, who became an American successful entrepreneur.

It is out of Art Williams' training that I came to value understanding. He taught me that "when you have done all that you can do, and you know that you have done all that you can do, only then will you have done enough." Usually when this concept sinks in, one's mental capacity "lights go off." I learned growing up that life is about choices and the ramifications of those choices. The ramifications often come much later than the individual choice, but they will come. As an educator, I have made efforts over the years to help others understand that there is a difference between a choice and a mistake. An entire volume could be devoted to this concept alone. How and when can we know we have done all that we can truthfully do? Knowing such keeps one from wallowing in doubt and self-pity.

Somewhere along the way, it dawned on me that to get something you never had, you have to do something that you have never done. I may have read this or heard it, but it made good sense to me. It suggests a commonsense approach to reality. It relates well to that above statement about insanity. It would seem that so many, especially in these times, believe they can acquire much more than they have by continuing to do the same thing over and over again. This principle can apply to a variety of concerns with life and living that life to its fullest.

Over the years, it has been my faith that has allowed me to survive. There have been so many challenges with heath issues, finances, and personal relationships. Were it not for my faith and grounding in the church, I am not sure how I would have managed to survive. There is that song of the church that says, "How I got over, my soul looks back and wonder how I got over." What principle of life can be drawn from this? Simply stated, "The will of God will never lead you where the grace of God will not protect you." One of the great songs of the faith assures us that "God will take care of you." My life's journey is a testimony to this. Over the decades, I have come to know that losing what would seem like everything changes nothing. I left home to attend Fisk University in Nashville, with not enough money to pay for a full semester of tuition, let alone to live in a dormitory and eat at the school's dining hall. Yet, I did these things when the odds seemed to be against me. I suppose out of this could come the cynical reply, "I have all that I need, except those things I do not have." But it is out of the abundance of God's grace that my basic needs have always been met.

I have now stated several affirmations that have sustained me over the years. These are to be used as focal points for describing the life of a poor, sickly, Black child, born in what would now be called the ghetto, who earned a PhD degree from Boston University in three years. This degree in biblical studies (the Hebrew Bible) required proficiency is seven languages. This child of the Depression did this and knows he has an obligation to share his faith with others. So, as told to others, he understands that for many he may be the only real Christian some will meet. The life and times of John W. Waters, PhD, has similarities to others whose lives have been enriched through their faith and commitment to bettering the world in which they exist wherever that might be. To God be the glory!

Chapter One
Education Begins

Education is a life-long process. Mine began in my home, where there was much reading and listening. My father was an avid reader, primarily to determine what "numbers" to play the next day. So, he read the Dow Jones Average, whether he understood this and the stock market or not. What he did know is that if he chose the right three numbers and played them, he would "hit the number." For a penny placed, he could win $4.50 playing the "number." Rarely did he win, but his interest drove him to purchase several newspapers, number books, etc., daily. So, to see him reading at night was routine. His lack of winning led me never to gamble virtually on anything. Both my parents left school in the sixth grade. Their parents were sharecroppers in middle Georgia. Sometimes they would share their experiences of having to leave school during planting and harvest. I never met any of my grandparents, whom all died before I was born.

Having brothers and sisters in school meant that there were schoolbooks around the house. As stated earlier, my mother would gather us and read to us. In addition, pestering my brothers and sisters who were in school, I learned to read and comprehend. We subscribed to *The Atlanta Constitution*, *The Atlanta Daily World*, and *The Pittsburg Courier*. I do not remember not being able to read or not having an interest in reading. At the top of the blackboard in my second-grade classroom was this quote: "Reading maketh a full man." Now it would have to read, "Reading makes a full person." Some would insist that it be politically correct.

The reading quote, I learned later, is from Francis Bacon's *Of Studies*. The complete quote is more determinate: "Reading maketh a full man; conference ready man; and writing an exact man." (Bacon, *Of Studies*, 1597). The writing aspect of this quote would seem to be where I am now in this life's journey.

My formal education began at the E. P. Johnson Elementary School, one of the Atlanta Board of Education's schools for colored children. Entering there in the first grade in January 1942, I graduated from the seventh grade in the spring of 1948. Yes, the seven grades were completed in six years. A grade was skipped for a number of reasons.

The only time my mother ever had to come to school to see about me was a time when I was in the fifth grade. The teacher, Miss Farnando, had asked me to read, which I did. She insisted that I do it louder. I told her I was reading as loudly as I could. Usually, I came home from school with a number of other children. My mother asked them where I was. She was told I had been kept after school. My mother walked from Peoplestown to Summer Hill to see what I had done that made the teacher keep me after school. When told that I refused to read loudly enough for her, my mother asked, did I read? She then responded by saying I was never to be kept after school again for such a reason, given that I was not a loud, noisy child. That was the only time in my tenure with the public schools of Atlanta that I was detained once the school day was over.

One of the unusual things about my elementary school was that all the teachers and principal were women. Even the superintendent of the Atlanta public school system was a woman, Dr. Ira Jarrell. She still held this position when I began my professional teaching career at David T. Howard High School. In this day and time, it may be hard to believe that only single women were allowed to teach in elementary schools here in Atlanta. My first male teacher was my eighth-grade homeroom teacher, Ralph Long. When I applied to the Atlanta system and was tentatively accepted, the final appointment would be made following an interview with Dr. Jarrell. At this interview, she assured me that I would have a high school science teaching position. It turned out to be a math and science position at Howard High School, where I had been a student for three years. Many on the faculty at that time had been there when I was a student.

My experience of going to E. P. Johnson from Peoplestown brings back both good and bad memories. Being poor often meant my shoes had cardboard in them from the holes. Clothes were often patched. I suppose this was true for many of us, especially since it was during the Depression. My father worked constantly during the War. Being a somewhat sickly child, it was easy for others to pick on me. It did not help that in most instances, I was thought to be the "brightest" child in a classroom. Remembering the name calling, insults, and fights on the way to and from school helped me to become quite independent and self-assured. This, too, has both positive and negative benefits. Learning to be on my own has resulted in some resistance to accepting help from others. So, even now, it is difficult to accept offers for assistance and gifts from others. There remains that constant desire to be truly independent even until death.

Elementary school was a half-day for me. Along with others, each day I walked almost two miles to school. Yes, I know each person my age walked "five" miles to school. During elementary school, and the first three years of high school, I never ate lunch, although it was served. My father never gave me any money to buy lunch. From around the age of nine, I worked after school with some men who lived in my neighborhood. One task was to pick up dry cleaning and laundry. Another was helping pick up cardboard boxes and paper. Several summers, I sold seeds in my neighborhood. None of these paid that much, but they provided me some money to purchase snacks and books for myself.

It was my resourcefulness that allowed me to take advantage of attending annual sessions of the Atlanta Symphony Orchestra (ASO) at the Atlanta City Auditorium. The schools allowed us to attend roughly every quarter. It was here that I was introduced first to classical music and the various instruments of an orchestra. We had a visiting music teacher who told us about the ASO and encouraged us to attend. I do not remember this teacher's name or most of my public-school teachers' names. Also, we had a library at the school, so I learned to take out books to take home to read. Later, I got a library card to the Auburn Avenue Library, one of the two public libraries in the city that "coloreds" were able to patronize. Such rigid, *de jure* segregation seems so long ago, but sometimes it seems like just yesterday.

My life as a child was spent helping around our home and "farming." Some do not remember that Atlanta has not always been a thriving urban center. There were out houses near the state capitol as I grew up. Subsequently, Capitol Homes, a public housing projects for whites only, changed the landscape of the area. My family, living in Peoplestown, south of downtown Atlanta, had use of land for gardening and raising hogs. When talking with others about my childhood, they seem surprised that I know so much about "farming." In reality, we had always a garden and raised chickens and hogs on land that did not belong to us. Others did the same. Nearby, on my street, were people who had goats, cows, rabbits, you name it. It was all on land that did not belong to any of us. So, the selling of seeds and other small jobs as a young child was not necessary out of the ordinary. Certainly, it was not for me.

My mother could grow almost anything. So, around our house, there were always plants. Our gardens would have a variety of vegetables including collard greens, corn, and beans. One house plant my mother had when I was a child I kept until 2013 when I downsized and moved into an apartment. Having green plants around was just a given. This appreciation I inherited from Mary Waters, my mother. My appreciation for punctuality is perhaps the only trait that I have from my father, Henry Waters.

The Atlanta public schools began a seven to five policy the year I attended the David T. Howard High School at 551 Houston St., NE,

Atlanta (now John Wesley Dobbs Ave). Most days, I walked almost three miles to attend school. The house where we lived in Peoplestown was put on the market. This was one of several duplexes owned by the same company along the same street, Farrington Avenue. My father said we could not afford to buy it. So, the family moved in with my mother's oldest sister in Summer Hill. We were there for almost a year. From there, 576 Terry St., I had to walk to David T. Howard because I could not afford to ride the streetcar, whose fare was just ten cents. Moving meant that I lost my "part time" jobs. The distance to Howard was about two and a half miles, which did not bother me since I was accustomed to walking. Walking is something I enjoy, and I suspect it has to do with having to do it as a young boy. The school day was from 9:00 a.m. to 3:00 p.m. Lunch was never an option. The semester's fee for high school was $2.50. Usually, it was near the end of the semester before my father would pay the fee. My father worked six or seven days per week for the same company, Atlanta Ice Company, for almost thirty years.

It was at E. P. Johnson Elementary School that I began to come into my own. I ran track, the 100-yard relay, and played "hockey" during recess. Perhaps the most significant thing was to become a safety patrol officer, which meant that there was a belt and badge that made a student standout from others with specific safety responsibilities. I kept the tradition into high school, where I became the "captain" of the safety patrol unit at Howard High School. During the ninth grade, our unit took a trip to Washington, D.C. for an annual convention of safety patrol officers, where I met President Harry S. Truman at the White House. Truman was one of three US presidents that I met. President Eisenhower was the second, and Jimmy Carter the third. President and Mrs. Carter came to Atlanta to work on a Habitat for Humanity housing complex. At that time, I was a board member of the Atlanta affiliate of the organization.

Each year of high school, I made the honor roll. Math and science were my best subjects, although in no course did I earn less than a B. It was during my high school years that my parents bought a home in the Dixie Hills area of Atlanta. At that time, this area was in Fulton County, unincorporated city of Atlanta. Although I lived here, on the West Side of the area, given that I had begun high school while living in Southeast Atlanta, I was allowed to remain a student at Howard High School. In reality, my residency was closer to Booker T. Washington High School, the first Black public high school in the city of Atlanta. However, given its reputation for violence, it was not where I wanted to be a student. The principal of David T. Howard High School, Charles Gideons, was a member of Allen Temple AME Church, where many of my relatives were members and where I had been involved in various youth activities. The relationship my family had with Mr. Gideons allowed me to remain a student at Howard High School in spite of the fact that I lived nearer Washington and should have been enrolled there.

The city of Atlanta annexed Dixie Hills and other areas. Fulton County was in the process of building both a high school and elementary school in Dixie Hills. In September 1951, the Henry McNeil Turner High School and the Anderson Park Elementary School opened in the same building. Since this had been designed as a Fulton County School for colored children, students from various sections of the county were enrolled, from the south side, Thomasville, west side, Adamsville, the north side, Roswell, etc. I transferred to Turner as an eleventh grade student and graduated in its first class in 1953, with honors in the top 5 percent of the class.

I suppose, in many ways, it was at Turner High that my life began to take the real shape of becoming a professional educator. Much of this just happened, some would say, through divine intervention. I was no longer that sickly boy from the Waters' family. But to tell this, there is need to go back to David T. Howard for a moment. Three areas studied there have had tremendous impacts on my life: wood shop, typing, and general business. Boys had to take wood shop and girls home economics regardless of interest. It was in wood shop that I learned skills in carpentry that have served me well. The typing skills allowed me to earn extra money through typing papers for others. The general business class taught me about banking and other financial matters. At Howard, for a free period, I signed up to work in the library. This, too, provided me with future revenue, especially as a college student. The late Dr. C. Eric Lincoln, noted Black sociologist, earned his master's degree at Fisk University. I had the privilege of typing his thesis.

As a student at Howard, among my classmates were Vernon Jordan, Lonnie King, Eldrin Bell, Margaret Matthews, and others who have played pivotal roles in the civil rights struggles. Attorney Vernon Jordan became an advisor to President Bill Clinton; Lonnie King was active in the Student Non-Violent Movement (SNCC) that led to the integration of public places in Atlanta and beyond. Eldrin Bell became, I believe, the first Black chief of police for the city of Atlanta and the first Black chairperson of the Clayton County Board of Commissioners. Margaret Matthew became an international track star. There are many others who were in the Howard High School Class of 1953, where I would have been had the city of Atlanta not annexed the Dixie Hills area.

Life can be strange for many reasons. One day, I saw a teacher at Howard who was so attractive that I thought whatever she was teaching, I would take. Mrs. Mamie Hubert taught Latin, so I took Latin as my elective simply because of her. I suppose in the back of my mind I knew I needed a foreign language because I was going to go to college, even though such a thought at the time would seem so remote. I had only one brother who had gone to college on the GI Bill, having served in World War II. He was a mechanical engineering major, a football jock at Florida Memorial College in St. Augustine, Florida. Six of my brothers served in the military during World War II. Only one used the GI Bill to further his education. A street in St. Augustine, Florida honors Fred Waters' memory as one of the first two Black policemen in that city and state.

I remember there were at least two vocational counselors at Howard. In my three years there as a student, neither ever advised me on any subject. My class schedules were arranged through my homeroom teachers and the scheduling committee. Again, it must have been through divine intervention that I had the desire to become a teacher, a career that would require me to attend college. Such desire also meant I had to be on the "college track" as a high school student. It was the electives chosen that assured me that I could attend college. Nothing in my socio-economic background could have suggested this to the counselors at Howard. Given that I was never a problem student, with almost perfect attendance and on the yearly honor roll, maybe they saw no reason to call me in for counseling or advising.

As indicated, after three years at Howard, I transferred to the new Henry McNeil Turner High School that was in walking distance of my home. Since Turner was new, courses that would have proved helpful to me were not offered. Latin was not an offering, so I took two years of French. German was offered, but it had no appeal to me. Turner had no chapter of the National Honor Society of which I would have become a member upon entering the eleventh grade had I remained at Howard. The only advanced math class offered was geometry. Initially at Turner, I was placed in an art class, home economics, choir, and woodshop. Eventually, I was able to move to take chemistry and geometry. Because of a reading of my transcript from Howard and a guidance counselor who took interest in the students at Turner, course changes for me were approved and implemented. That counselor, Francis Long, played a pivotal role in my education and future.

Looking back at my high school yearbook, even I am surprised at the number of extra-curricular activities in which I participated. I counted seven, ranging from writing for the newspaper, playing cornet in the band, to serving as president of the Tri-Hi-Y, and the school bank. Through an arrangement with the Fulton Federal Bank, a student bank was set up at our school. This introduced me to the Junior Chamber of Commerce, as well as provided a place to save my money from a part-time, after-school job.

Perhaps two interesting experiences came out of course work. As a student in American history with Mr. B. S. Burch, I was invited by him to become a part of a group known as "Experts on Current Events." Many would call this Turner's Debate Team. And as a member of the Red Cross Apprentices program, the work of the American Red Cross was made clearer to me and to others. This association took me to McClendon Hospital, one of several private Black hospitals in Atlanta. So, over the years, I have continued to be a consistent supporter of the American Red Cross. At McClendon, I met Black physicians who had medical degrees from prominent medical schools from around the world. All the medical care I had received came from the colored Grady Hospital, where there were Black nurses but virtually no Black physicians. During this time, the state of Georgia paid the tuition of Black students to attend medical schools outside of the state.

Earlier, I mentioned Francis Long, a counselor at Turner. Mr. Long was a PhD student at the University of Michigan, studying psychometrics. He formed a group of ten to twelve students to teach them the art of test taking. This group met at his home every Saturday for at least a semester. For some reason, again divine intervention, I was one of those students. Mr. Long used "old" SAT tests to teach us the skills of test taking. Because of this, my studying of Latin, and being good in math, when I took the SAT, I scored a 1540 out of a possible 1600. Subsequently, when required to take the ACT for grad school, I scored thirty-four out of a possible thirty-six. Once completing my college degree and taking the National Teachers' Exam in science, I scored in the 92nd percentile. Much of this I owe to the insight of Francis Long, a guidance counselor who took a real interest in students regardless of their socio-economic background.

In one of the hymns of the church, I look back and wonder "How I got over." Again, it had to have been through divine intervention that all this and more took place in the life of a Black boy from the "ghetto," who did not know others saw in him what he did not see or recognize within himself.

It would be easy to suggest at this point that life for me as a student always went well. Such was not the case.

Chapter Two
Do Not Let That Which You Cannot Do...

I suppose my first real disappointment as an energetic and intelligent student came in my tenth grade English class, taught by Mrs. Anna Jackson (Grant). One of the assignments was to write an essay. I do not remember what the subject was to be. I spent time in the library researching the subject, completed the paper, which was not a term paper. The course was titled English Composition. A few days later, I got the paper back with a notation that it was not mine given the maturity of the thought and writing style. If memory serves me correctly, in both the eighth and ninth grade English classes, my final grade was an A. Yet, Mrs. Jackson insisted the paper had not been written by me. At the time, I did not know the term "plagiarism." She insisted that I submit another paper, which I did. I do believe my final grade from Mrs. Jackson was a B+. It could have been an A. She came to see that John Waters did possess some good writing and research skills. After all, I served as a librarian assistant.

Perhaps one of my most disheartening moments came during a visit to an aunt, my mother's oldest sister, Ludie Odom. I had driven my mother to Aunt Ludie's, who was ailing at the time. Standing next to her bed, beside my mother, my aunt looked at me and told my mother that I should leave high school and get a job because my future did not look promising. At the time, I was a junior in high school and an honor student. But my aunt said, "Bay," the name she called my mother, "you just wait and see." Of course, I did not leave high school. Aunt Ludie had fourteen children, all of whom finished high school; some went to college, but none received a degree. At that time, my mother had only one child who had finished college. Aunt Ludie did not have a single child or grandchild who had earned a degree higher than a master's degree. My mother, on the other hand, has me, the first in the family to earn a PhD, and three additional offspring who have also earned PhD degrees. In our family, there is a history of professional educators, beginning with me.

An interesting and educational incident occurred in my geometry class. Mr. E. T. Lewis had a reputation as an excellent teacher. One day, as he was putting and explaining a geometric theorem on the board, I stopped him to tell him he had made a mistake in the deduction of the theorem. Mr. Lewis started shaking and then said, "After some twenty-plus years in teaching, no student has ever caught me making a mistake." When I explained to him what the mistake in deduction had been, he admitted he had made an error. This for me was a valuable learning experience: as a teacher, never present yourself as perfect. When I became a teacher, I would, and still do, make "errors," just to see if there are those paying attention. And when I do make an error, the students do not know whether such is intentional or my just "joking around."

The most grievous thing to happen to me as a high school student was not realized until after my commencement. Report cards could only be picked up following commencement, since the semester was not officially over for a week after receiving the diploma. In all the courses taken that final semester, I had earned A's, with the exception of English, where the indicated grade was a C. I could make no sense of this given that for all the exams and tests taken in the English class, my lowest grade was a 92. It dawned on me, for the first time, that teachers are not always fair. Several weeks before graduation in the English class, Mrs. B. J. Tipton asked us where we planned to attend college. When it came to me, I said I planned to go to Emory. She told me how ridiculous this was given that Emory did not admit Black students. Never being one afraid to talk back, I told her how narrow-minded and shortsighted she was, and that no teacher should ever say such to anyone. This was the only way to justify receiving a C in a class where my lowest grade had been an A. When I told my mother why I had a C in English and showed her all my paperwork from the class, we went to Turner to speak with Mr. Davis, the principal. Needlessly to say, Mary Waters was "angry as hell." We showed Mr. Davis my report card and all the papers from Mrs. Tipton's class. He said he would take care of the matter. The next day, we received a call from him saying Mrs. Tipton had made a mistake in her calculations and that my final grade was a B. This did not make the situation right, but it taught me the lesson that prejudice can be found in many forms. Unfortunately, Mrs. Tipton received her master's in counseling and became a guidance counselor with the Atlanta public school system.

Mrs. Tipton was right. I did not attend Emory; I did not even apply. I was admitted to Stanford and Columbia universities, although now it is not clear why I would have thought I could afford to attend either. In the early 1990s, Boston University asked me to serve as its official representative to the installation service of the Dean of the Candler School of Religion at Emory. Prior to graduating from Turner, I received four-year scholarships offers from nearly every Black college in Georgia, including Morehouse College, where Principal Davis wanted me to attend. Morehouse was his alma mater. At the time, I knew nothing of the ROTC programs at Tuskegee and Hampton Institutes. Looking back, I probably would have gone to one of these given that the cost would have been less than what it cost to attend Fisk. I did not attend Emory, but through the course of my education, I attended Fisk University, Atlanta University, the University of Detroit, the University of Geneva, and Boston and Harvard universities.

In the eleventh grade, I got a part time job working at Sunshine Department Store. My mother had worked on and off as a domestic for the Sunshine family. She got me the job. I began there as a stock boy and janitor daily and sometimes on a Sunday when a special sale was to take place. Sunshine had several locations; I worked at the main store at 795 Marietta St., NW, Atlanta. Over time, I learned alterations, pricing of merchandise, etc. Slowly, Mr. Harry Sunshine, the owner, began allowing me to sell to the Black customers. The Sunshines were Jews who had migrated from Russia. Having obtained a driver's license at the age of 16, eventually Mr. Sunshine would have me pick up merchandise from various vendors and deliver it to his other stores. He found me reliable, dependable, and trustworthy. He offered to pay for me to attend college if I would major in economics and come back to work for him.

After graduating high school, Mr. Sunshine gave me a full-time job for the summer. He paid me what he paid his other salespeople, all of whom were white. Mrs. Sunshine objected to this, so he told me that in order to keep the peace with his wife and other employees, he would have to reduce my salary but not my work responsibilities. About the same time, one of the white salesclerks invited me to visit her at her home on Ponce de Leon Avenue. I told my parents, who recognized the same thing I did—such was not tolerated in the South in those days. We thought it best that I quit my job at Sunshine's, and I did. One of my brothers was a longtime employee at Alterman Brothers, a major food distributor and food store owner in the South. So, the very next week after quitting Sunshine Department Stores, I had a job with Alderman Brothers. There I worked as a stock boy and learned to operate a folk lift machine. I worked there until late summer, when I departed Atlanta for Nashville and enrolled as a freshman at Fisk University.

My interest in music led my oldest sister to buy me a piano. A neighbor taught beginning piano. So, around the age of 14 or 15, Felmore Baugh was my piano teacher. When he had taught me all he could, he referred me to his piano teacher, Mary Shy, who lived in Grady Homes, a public housing project for Blacks in the fourth ward area of the city. I tell this only because after leaving Felmore's tutelage, a couple times he took me to the movies with him. We lived in Dixie

Hills and, in order to ride the bus, we had to walk through some woody areas and a portion of Lincoln Cemetery. One late evening, as we were returning from the movies and in the wooded area, he tried to seduce me. Of course, I resisted. I did not tell my parents about this, even after my mother asked me why I stopped going places with Felmore, who seemed such a fine young man. This experience taught me that attempted seduction of a young boy did not only occur with women but also with other men. Similar incidents, primarily with women, occurred throughout my life. One ninth-grade boy, after a class that I was teaching, came to me and said he always got his way with men. I told him not with this one. He was in my ninth-grade science class. A female junior at the Interdenominational Theological Center, who had been assigned as one of my advisees, told me what she wanted to do with me before she graduated. It was clear what she had in mind. From this experience, I always kept my office door open whenever there was someone in the office with me. The year the young lady graduated (and by now she had married), she stopped by to tell me what I had "missed." Divine intervention.

I finished high school in May 1953. In June of that year, my father was murdered. One evening, after my oldest sister had left her first husband and moved back home, her estranged husband, James Harris, forced his way into our home and fired several rounds off through one of our doors. At the time, both my father and I were home. Vivian had run into my parents' bedroom, where the rest of the family was. The door was closed, so James shot through the door. Once inside, my father tackled him and was shot during the ensuing scuffle. While James wrestled with my father, I took one of my mother's kerosene lamps and knocked him out. We called the police and James was still unconscious when they arrived. My father was rushed to Grady Hospital, where he later died. James was tried and convicted of first-degree murder. With so much drama, my mother decided that I could not go far away from home. So, having been accepted at Fisk University in Nashville, there is where I enrolled. I told my mother that I would not attend college in

Georgia. Looking back, the details of what caused me to arrive at that decision are not that clear, except I knew that I had to leave home.

These recounted incidents have never been regarded as being unique to me. Over the years, I have discovered that there are those who will go out of their way to entice you to violate personal values. That said, I have not lived a prefect life and avoided all temptations. Sometimes I tell people that the Bible mentions only two perfect people and neither of them were named John.

"Don't let that which you cannot do keep you from doing what you can." John Wooden

Chapter Three
When You Have Done All That You Can...

At this point in my life, it is sometimes necessary to tell people that life for me has not always gone well. As a professional, some assume that the environment out of which I came had to be at least middle class. When this has happened to me, the usual response is to quote the first several lines from Langston Hughes' *Mother to Son*.

> "Well son, I'll tell you.
> Life for me ain't been no crystal stair.
> It's had tacks in it, and splinters,
> And boards torn up.
> And places with no carpet on the floor—
> Bare."

Even though my father was murdered the year I finished high school, neither his life nor death would have discouraged me from attending college. I had saved some money for college, but his death, actually was able to help me achieve my goal. My mother's attorney, Francis Fife, told her about the Social Security benefits to which I would be entitled. So, beginning my sophomore year of college, I received a monthly Social Security check that helped with my expenses. However, from my first week as a freshman at Fisk, I worked in the library and did so through graduation.

Attending Fisk was primarily a way of getting out of Georgia. The oldest Black college in the South, Fisk had a reputation of catering to Black elites. Some referred to it as the "Harvard of the South." It seems almost like yesterday that I was filling out the admission application. In addition to standard information, it requested information about the number of bedrooms in my home and whether we had indoor bathrooms. I'm not sure that had I confessed we had an outhouse and a number two tin tub for bathing that I would have been admitted. Given that Fisk was just across the street from Meharry Medical College, one of the two Black medical schools at that time, many of its students were pre-med majors. Some of the young women made it clear that their parents had sent them to Fisk to land a Meharry man as a husband. I was not a pre-med major or from a prominent Black family, as were some others who had graduated from public schools across the country.

Working in the library at Fisk and being a chemistry major left little time for a social life. I began my work in the library as a student assistant who helped others locate materials. The starting pay was forty-five cents per hour. Remember, the year was 1953. Having worked in libraries from my high school days, I understood the Dewey Decimal and Congressional Library cataloging systems. This skill, along with having mastered bookkeeping skills in a general business course taken in high school, helped me end up serving as the "accountant" for the library before the end of my freshman year. One of the regular staff members resigned, leaving this position open. I informed my supervisor that I could handle this position, and after demonstrating proficiency at this, the position was given to me. My salary increased to ninety cents per hour and I had keys to the library and its various collections, among which was the largest collection about Negroes in the world. Many of my free hours were spent researching in this unique collection. Even now, after all these years, others seemed to be impressed by my knowledge of Black literature, its history, and writers.

Turner High awarded me a tuition scholarship to Fisk; the amount I do not recall. The school sent the check to Fisk. The school responded to Mr. Davis, the principal, pointing out how much I needed financial assistance. Mr. Davis sent me a copy of the letter. Note, I worked at Fisk from my first week there until I graduated from there within four years without incurring any debt. Given what Fisk did, it was many, many years before I could bring myself to support my alma mater. Even to this day, it bothers me to think that an institution dedicated to the advancement of Black people would do such a thing.

This chapter opened with a quote from Langston Hughes, a writer and poet out of the Harlem Renaissance period. The head of the Fisk University Library during my student days was Arna Bontemps, noted Harlem Renaissance poet and writer. Also at Fisk was Aaron Douglas, noted Black artist from this period. He was my art history professor. It was at Fisk that I came to appreciate the tradition of the Fisk Jubilee Singers, under the direction of John W. Works.

Attending college during the days of the Cold War had both positive and negative consequences. This was the McCarty era—there were "witch hunts" for "communists" across the United States. A number of white college professors, thought to be communists for numerous reasons, lost their teaching positions at northern predominately white colleges and universities. Many of these ended up in the South at Black institutions of higher learning. Two such were Robert and Gertrude Rempfer, both who had PhD degrees and had taught at Temple University. Dr. Gertrude Rempfer's field was physics, and she was one of the co-inventors of the electronic microscope. Dr. Robert Rempfer was a noted mathematician. One year, the Rempfers had sublet their home to a Black couple. This was in violation of Temple's housing policy. This proved them to be "communists," and they were fired. Fisk hired both in their fields of expertise. Both were teachers of mine. In Nashville, the Rempfers created a stir when they sought to enlist their white children in the nearby all Black school. To many, this proved that they were either socialists or communists. In either case, for me, both were excellent and gifted professors from whom I took courses and frequently visited their home near the campus.

My years at Fisk were filled with a variety of student-oriented activities. Having my Fisk yearbook with me, the thought occurred to look to see if I could find some activities in which I had been involved. The listing beside my name included: "Apprentice Club; Stagecrafters; Forum; Oval; Chemistry Club; Men's Senate; NAACP; F.I.S.C. Co-coordinator; American Chemical Society; Student Affiliate of American Chemical Society; Math Club; Art Workshop; and Chairman of Livingstone Hall Open House Committee." In several of these, I served as an officer from president, secretary, and treasurer. Participation with the NAACP led me, along with other Fiskites, to protest the segregated public transportation system in Nashville. In my senior year, I served as vice-president of the campus chapter of the NAACP and until this day, continue to hold a membership in this civil rights organization.

Looking back over the activities available to students, I am reminded that I did not participate in any of the religious or Greek organizations. Most Sundays, I attended church or chapel on campus or at a local nearby Baptist church. The chapel music was always excellent, but I did not participate in its choir. As a chemistry major and worker on campus, there was little time for the extracurricular activities the college had to offer. Now, I realize it was a mistake not to take time to be a part of at least one of the religious organizations on campus, such as the Baptist Student Union. Joining a Black Greek-letter organization was something that I knew I could not afford, so there was no need to pursue such even if there was an interest. I have no significant regrets for missing out on many things at Fisk.

Fisk did, however provid me with many cultural experiences. Of course, the Jubilee Singers' concerts were always exceptional. Through the cultural affairs program, I heard my first production of Shakespeare's Hamlet and several performances by the Canadian Players, including Peer Gynt. There was the appearance of Alyne Dumas Lee, soprano; Mattiwilda Dobbs, soprano; Pro Musica Antiqua; E. Power Biggs, organist; and many well-known artists of the times. Many Saturdays, I listened to the Metropolitan Opera via radio, sponsored by Texaco. It was also here that I was introduced to the School of Theology at Boston University. One of our chapel speakers was Dr. Allan Knight Chalmers, professor of homiletics at Boston. His sermon, "Your

Signature," was in my mind when I applied to the two seminaries where I had some interest.

At the Senior Awards Day, I received the school's journalism award. One of my freshmen classes was public speaking. Its instructor was Miss Fannie Bennett. One day following class, Miss Bennett asked me if I had ever written poetry. To this day, I am not sure what prompted her question. Her suggestion led to my first published poem, "The Great Awakening," which the university published in its national alumni magazine. I was also on the editorial board of the newspaper.

Some of my more interesting experiences at Fisk occurred in its Little Theater. Miss Bennett was an instructor in Dramatics. She left Fisk at the end of my freshman year to pursue an acting career in New York.

As a high school student, I had participated on a rather limited schedule in drama. At Fisk, this became a major interest that extended through my senior year. The Stagecraters was the student acting group under the direction of Dr. Lillian Voorhees and Dr. Gladys Forde. Working here, I learned about the production side of presenting plays. Makeup and building sets were both interesting and challenging. My carpentry skills and knowledge of electricity were helpful. I had several acting roles. I remember playing several minor roles in Shakespeare's *Julius Caesar* and Tennessee Williams' *Cat on a Hot Tin Roof.* Major acting roles were given almost exclusively to those students whose parents made significant financial contributions to the school. One student's parent, also a Fisk alum, gave the school a grand piano, others were trustees, etc. My only claim to fame was the passion to become an educator.

Each year that I was at Fisk, I returned to Atlanta during the summer months and found work. One summer, my job was a construction worker on daily assignments. This was probably the most physically demanding job I ever had. It paid well, so I endured it just to have money for school. One summer, I worked for the Atlanta Public Water Works. I learned to install water meters, use a jack hammer, lay out pipes, and repair broken water lines. So, I have a public servant component to my past. I never felt any job was beneath me, knowing that it was always temporary and that each was a step toward becoming that professional teacher.

My four years at Fisk provided meaningful opportunities for several reasons. One was simply meeting and studying under Dr. John R. Cottin, professor of French. Dr. Cottin was my French instructor for two years. Perhaps more than French, I learned and adopted one of his sayings: "Let not society dictate your values." This is my mantra for whom I have become. My primary chemistry instructor, Dr. Samuel Massie, had several of his organic chemistry students assist him on a navy research project, and I was one of the chosen students. Dr. Massie left Fisk and became the first Black professor at the US Navy Academy in Annapolis, Maryland.

Chapter Four
When You Have Done All That... (Part 2)

My senior year at Fisk had me taking education courses to become a certified teacher. I sent out numerous letters seeking employment as a high school science teacher. One of the first responses was from the Atlanta public school system. It had been my desire from my high school days to teach science at one of Atlanta's public schools. As mentioned previously, I had an interview with its then superintendent, Dr. Ira Jarrell.

In August 1957, I began working as a science and math teacher at the David T. Howard High School, which had the nickname "Hell's Kitchen." It was the second public high school established for Atlanta's Black students. Carver High had opened earlier, but it was an exclusively vocational high school. Washington High, the oldest public high school for Blacks, was on the west side of the city, and Howard was on the east side. There were sometimes violent rivalries between these schools. At that time, Washington had approximately five thousand students and Howard had three thousand.

Most of the faculty members at Howard had been there when I was a student. This presented some problems for them. They had to accept that I was a faculty member, no longer a student. This sounds easier than it was—a twenty-one-year-old who returned to teach where he and some of his siblings had been students.

During the first semester, I was assigned to teach two science classes, two math classes, and one spelling class. Each class was held in a different classroom and on a different floor of the U-shaped building. Most times, I had to rush to get from one class to the other before the students. Given that I was new, one of my general science classes had a fair number of football players. At the end of that semester, most received a failing grade. Never again in my three years at Howard did I have many student athletes. In my third year, students in the human anatomy class staged a rebellion against the instructor. She was removed from this class, and it was assigned to me. She, in turn, took one of my science classes.

One semester during my Howard High teaching assignment, I had a general science class for "slow learners." Today, such students would be classified as children with learning disabilities or students with special needs. These students never presented a problem simply because the course work was reduced to their individual level. They were taught to look at simple things such as leaves and rocks and to learn what made these objects different. They were asked to design science projects reflecting their interest. Each was given an opportunity to present their project to their classmates. In those days, it would seem the teacher had more discretion in presenting material than is now true in the public school system of Atlanta.

At Howard, I became known as a strict disciplinarian. This reputation still follows me. It served me well since there were few behavioral problems with students. The principal designated me as a "model teacher." So, as a third-year instructor, I received tenure and was also assigned a student teacher, a young math major from Spelman College. In my third year at Howard, the Atlanta public school system introduced the use of television in its public schools. Howard named me to serve on a science committee to prepare presentations on television for high school students. This sponsorship by the Board of Education led to the now PBA-30, a national public broadcast outlet in Atlanta. This initial project was sponsored by the Ford Foundation.

Each year as a science teacher, I encouraged students to participate in the annual public schools' science fair. My students participated in the colored school science fairs. I participated in the Atlanta Science Teachers Association, where I became its secretary. This provided an opportunity to work with the science teachers from across the city. Each year, at least one of my students would be the recipient of a science student award.

Part of my regular teaching schedule at Howard was a spelling class. This I did for two years. Out of this came the publication *Some Modern Trends in Spelling Instruction: A Guide for Teachers of Spelling*, 1957. This guide, a major portion submitted by me, was used in the colored public high schools of Atlanta.

A student, Herbert J Bridgewater, Jr., who was assigned to one of my spelling classes, was there for only one day. He was a junior. For some reason, he decided to ask me to help him in his campaign to become the student council president. The annual campaign allowed juniors to run for president and vice president of the student council, taking office in their senior year. At Howard, for a number of years, one of the social science teachers, Melvin Waples, had been the sponsor of the winning candidate. Even after these many years, it is not clear to me why this young man thought I could help him win his campaign. But win he did by a very large margin. To do this, a winning strategy was put in place with a variety of activities that assured the young man of getting real name recognition among the entire student population. I worked with him on speech preparation, fund raising, etc. Having won, he was told that for the student council banquet he could invite his parents and one other person. He chose to invite another faculty member from the social science department as the other guest. She had done little, if anything, as a part of his campaign. From this, I learned that investing in someone else is a good idea, even if the investee fails to realize what has occurred. I do hope that those who went out of their way to invest their time and energy in me did not get the negative result that I did from my single experience with high school politics.

My tenure as a high school science and math instructor was interrupted by serving in the US military. In the days of the draft, I was classified as 1-A. In my third year at Howard, I received my draft notice that would require me to serve in the US Army for two years. Instead, in June of 1960, I volunteered for a three-year tour of duty with the understanding that this would be served in Europe, and it was. When I finished my tour and returned to teach in Atlanta, I was assigned to teach science at the Luther J. Price High School in southeast Atlanta. There, I taught four classes, two in biology and two in physics. That summer, the teacher who had taught physics at Price High School died. This was my last year of teaching for the Atlanta public school system. Returning from the US Army, I made the decision to enter a graduate theological program in New England.

It was during my three years tenure at Howard High School that my life took on a relatively dark side. This, too, contributed to my volunteering for the US Army. A neighborhood friend, a year or so older than me, led me willingly to the verge of being an alcoholic. Freddie Morgan, who lived up the street from me, did not attend Turner High. Given that the year Turner opened he was a senior at Booker T. Washington, there he remained. It was only after finishing college and returning to teach in Atlanta that we became friends. Looking back, this may have occurred because I owned a car and he did not. We became running partners, staying out late at night almost every night and night club jumping. It's hard to believe now, but at that time I dated two faculty members at Howard at the same time. One of the ladies lived nearby, and I drove her to Howard every morning. The other lived in the southeast section of the city in south Atlanta.

Barbara Lovinggood had been a majorette at Turner High School. She was a class behind me and had been a student at Booker T. Washington High School. She lived in Dixie Hills, as I did. Barbara went to Clark

College, now Clark-Atlanta University, and majored in French. Upon graduation from Clark, she became one of the French teachers at Howard as well as director of the cheerleaders and majorettes at the school. We became quite close, and many assumed that the two of us would marry. As mentioned above, at the same time, I was dating another faculty member at Howard. Looking back over my life some years ago, it became clear to me that I was not ready to be married for many reasons. My relationship with Freddie and our lifestyle and the pressure to get married contributed to my volunteering for the military. At least, this is what I have believed over the years. I never filed for a deferment, although I had many reasons for doing so. But back to what must be seen as a continuation of my darker side.

On non-date nights, sometimes we double-dated. Freddie and I just hung out at various night spots until their closing time. The closest I ever came to being arrested was an evening that I had not gone with Freddie to one of the VFW Black oriented clubs in Atlanta. These remained open past the 2:00 a.m. closing time for Fulton County adult entertainment places. The VFW on Fair Street was noted for gambling, which was illegal in Atlanta.

One evening, not feeling well, I remained home. Around 4:00 a.m., I received a call from Freddie, who had been booked at the Atlanta City jail along with all those present at the VFW that evening. He had not been gambling, as I would not have been either, but he was present. So, I went down that morning and bonded him out. Freddie was into fashion designs and decided to relocate to New York. He tried to convince me to move there with him. Seeing my life wasting away, I declined and instead volunteered for the Army to go to Europe since I was 1-A and was scheduled to be drafted. I visited Freddie in Brooklyn on many occasions because we were dear friends. It was at Freddie's that I met Lorraine Hansberry, the playwright and author of the award winning *A Raisin in the Sun*, along with other artists from various dance and theatric groups. Unfortunately, Freddie's lifestyle did not change and in his late forties, he succumbed to cirrhosis of the liver.

One of the better decisions I made for myself was to volunteer for the US Army with the stipulation that I would serve in Europe. In December 1960, I arrived in Regensburg West Germany and remained stationed in West Germany until June 1963. Although I had not been a history major in college, it was of great interest to me. Much of my studying of it centered on Europe and its contributions to Western civilization.

My basic training took place at Ft. Jackson, S.C. I am not sure what I thought would happen during this training period. Most of the young men in my units were around the age of eighteen. Given that I had finished college and taught school for three years, I was one of the oldest trainees. I had not been that physically active through high school or college, given the need and necessity to work. The rigor of getting into shape for the military started from day one at Ft. Jackson. The day began around 4:30 a.m. with exercise, then off to breakfast and the routine of molding somewhat undisciplined young men into responsible soldiers with basic military skills.

From a single day I came to realize why Ft. Jackson was often referred to as the "Hell Hole of the Army." The temperature and humidity were almost unbearable during the June–July period of the training. Enduring the humiliation from drill sergeants and others took patience that I did not know I had. The thought of doing something to get out never came to my mind. Weaponry training, map reading, and other mental tasks were easy to master. Serving on KP duty and policing the grounds were often de-humanizing, but I did them without complaints. Weekends off with a pass allowed me to visit places near the base.

Only on one weekend did I return home to Atlanta. Upon completion of basic training, I was sent to Ft. Benning, Georgia, for Advance Infantry Training. Even today, people find it strange that I would have served in the infantry. I remind them that I volunteered for the Army. It was advance training in several areas, including weapons, where I became a sharp-shooter. Ft. Benning is located just outside of Columbus, Georgia. It was at Ft. Benning that I witnessed several recruits terminated for a variety of reasons. One day on the rifle training range, one soldier in training attempted to fire on a target and turned his rife toward an officer, pulling its trigger, and saying that it would not fire. This young man was immediately taken from the site and was never seen again. We were told he had psychological problems and issued a dishonorable discharge. Others lost their "cool" during various maneuvers and had to repeat the training cycle or were discharged.

Fort Benning is home to many well-known divisions of the US Army. Its location near the Georgia and Alabama state lines allowed for contact from furloughs for short periods of time. Many have heard of the location of a War College there, where many foreign personnel came to be trained. The history of General George Patton at Ft. Benning and his influence on the Army and the area are legendary.

I spent several Saturdays and Sundays in the Columbus area. I had a college classmate, Harry Stephens, who grew up there and was teaching at Spencer High School. Through him my weekends in the Ft. Benning area were filled with a variety of activities. Given the close proximity to Atlanta, I made several trips back home. It was at Ft. Benning that I discovered a taste for 3.5 beer served on base. My drinking returned on weekend furloughs. Once the training at Ft. Benning was completed, my unit, along with others, were flown to Ft. Ord, New Jersey, for deployment to Europe. This was the first time I had been on an airplane. The trip to Germany took eight or nine days on the USS Patch. Here, I learned what it means to be seasick. Given my interest in music and religion, I served as the organist for religious services on board. It was this trip to Europe on a military cargo ship that made me realize that ship or boat travel was not something that I would enjoy. At the end of the somewhat turbulent trip, I arrived in West Germany.

I could have been stationed at any US Army base in Europe. I was stationed at Neu Ulm, Wiley Barracks, West Germany, not far from Stuttgart, West Germany. Volunteering meant that I would spend three years in service rather than the two required under the draft law at the time.

Neu Ulm is in Bavaria, near the Swabian Alps. It is a small neighboring city of Ulm. Ulm's Ulm Minister has the tallest church steeple in the world. It is situated on the Danube River and is the home of Albert Einstein. This picturesque location is where I spent most of my enlisted days. I had vacations, but I never returned to the States for one of these. I spent many weekends traveling around this area visiting historical cities, castles, churches, etc. For each local region, there was always a church with a high steeple that was at the center of the area. Neuschwanstein Castle (1869–1892), also known as Fairytale Castle or the Castle of the Swan, where King Ludwig II, king of Bavaria, built an unusual castle, was the most beautiful castle I have yet to see.

I am getting ahead of myself and will return to my life in the military and how much of a positive influence it has had on me, and still does. Often, I am caught talking to others about the lack of respect for authority and discipline. Both are characteristics of the military at the time when I served. As indicated previously, other than two training cycles, one at Ft. Jackson and the other at Ft. Benning, my military career was served in the small West German town of Neu Ulm.

While serving in the army, I had a MOS classification as a mechanic. I suppose this happened given the Army's aptitude test and my training as a chemist. Life has had a way of opening doors and opportunities for me even until this day. While a student at Fisk University, one of the master's students in psychology asked me to take the Stanford-Binet IQ test, which I did. On this, I scored a 136. This was the first indication to me that I had some innate intellectual ability. The Army gave its Army Alpha test, which scored me with an IQ of 146—a farther confirmation that the SAT and the Stanford test results were somewhat accurate. Given that my Army record contained such information and that I had been a schoolteacher, soon after arriving at Neu Ulm, I was assigned as the administrator of that base education center. Most of my military career, served in West Germany, was served as an administrator of an Army education center.

When You Have Done All That ... (Part 2)

The director of the center, John McClain, allowed me much latitude in caring out the functions as one of its two administrators. The other administrator, Norris Hogan, a draftee, and I had taught at the same high school in Atlanta. The secretary, Frauline Liselotte Ortlieb, saw to it that the affairs of the center were always in order. Frauline Ortlieb and I remained in communication for some forty years after my departure from Germany. As I grew older and moved into a senior citizen home, I stopped getting her usual long letters at Christmas. As with so many others, she is counted as one of those persons who through divine intervention came into my life.

It was here that the base commander recommended me for Officers Candidate School (OCS), which would require me to re-enlist for four more years. This I did not do, and I have no regrets. My enlistment purpose was to go to Europe. While stationed there, I traveled to several countries, including Austria, Belgium, Czechoslovakia, Poland, and others. I was able to attend two summer sessions at the University of Geneva and almost a month traveling behind the Iron Curtain.

It was through a close friendship with a fellow soldier who worked in personnel that I was able to have sufficient furlough time to study in Switzerland and travel to several communist countries. Both required having a passport, which, as a military person, I did not have. After an appeal made to US Senator Richard Russell (D-Ga.), my passport was secured. I could not go to Russia as US soldier. So, I went there as part of the Munich American High School faculty. It was this trip to Russia, while Nikita Khrushchev served as premier of the Soviet Union, that took me to several communist controlled countries, including Poland. Getting into Russia was an ordeal unto itself.

The weeks I spent at the University of Geneva proved both difficult and interesting. All the courses were taught in French. These made me recall some of my French studies from both high school and college. The University of Geneva is one of the oldest universities in Europe. Geneva was a most beautiful and clean city. Here, I learned much about Switzerland, its culture, and people. Soon I discovered that the

Swiss, like the Mexicans, took the afternoon off. Those occupying the streets between noon and 4:00 p.m. were, for the most part, tourists. Such clean and sanitary streets I had never witnessed before. There are many national offices in Geneva, including that of the World Health Organization (WHO). Being interested in history and world affairs, I visited many of these, along with churches and museums. Geneva is said to be one of the most expensive cities in the world in which to live.

My trip to Geneva was solely to attend the French Summer Program at the university. As with many places in Europe at that time, you could go to a city and at the train station find local housing with a family. The family I lived with was German speaking Swiss, although they now lived in the French speaking section of the country. Herr and Frau Saegesser lived on Rue Colonel Coutan in Geneva, not far from the university. So, almost daily, I walked from their home to my classes, which were over by noon. They provided breakfast and dinner as a part of the expense charged to me as a resident in their home. Most days, I had lunch at a local café or restaurant.

The Swiss are known for mountain climbing. Posted around the university were endless signs about weekend climbs. Being a solider and thinking that I was in excellent physical condition, I signed up for a day trip and climb for one of the Saturdays I was in Geneva. That was a big mistake! I got to the train station early and boarded along with maybe twenty-five or so students. The train took us to the base of a mountain. We departed. Our guide gave out detailed information about the mountain path and how to get to the summit. We were told it would require more energy coming down the mountain than getting up it. We were also told the beautiful sight we would see from the top of the mountain. I do remember getting to the top. I do not remember the sight. We descended the mountain and took a ferry back to Geneva. I remember getting home late that Saturday. My next memory was waking up mid-day the following Monday. My hosts took care of this "physically fit" soldier those hours without him being aware that he had lost consciousness. I remember the ferry ride back to have taken so long that to this day, I have not ventured on one.

When my two summer sessions were over, I returned to West Germany and my responsibilities as an administrator for an education center. Of course, there were the numerous requests to share my experiences with others and questions about how, as a soldier, this had been possible.

There are so many positive experiences to recall from my time spent in the military. One that was most delightful had to do with my role at the Army Education Center. As a part of its educational advancement program in Europe, every so often, there would be what was the equivalent of a commencement exercise. Robert McClain, who was the director of the center where I was stationed, was invited as a special guest to the military headquarters facility of USAREUR (the Seventh Army) at Heidelberg, West Germany. He invited me to accomplish him. We camped along the banks of the Neckar River near downtown Heidelberg. The scenery was magnificent. The commencement took place in the courtyard of the castle where the headquarters was located.

It would be a tremendous oversight on my part if I did not mention my contact and association with the Slovak Gospel Mission. This association had its primary focus getting Bibles to Christians who lived in countries behind the Iron Curtain. My friend John Dalen, an insurance agent of Mr. McClain, introduced me to this group. Knowing of its work and mission, I spent time securing and getting the requested Bibles and Christian literature to those whose very lives were being put in danger because of their religious convictions and the belief of their governments that they were subversives who were out to overthrow their communist leaders. This involvement reflected my commitment to the church at a time when "the church" behind the Iron Curtain was constantly under attack. I got into reading about resistance movements, the work of atheist governments, and the reality that to be a Christian could be costly. As I reflect on what motivated me to Christian ministry, surely this association would have to be considered a part of it. It may have been during my association with this ministry that the desire to attend seminary and a graduate theological school came to me. Even after all these years, I still cannot give a defensive response to how and why I was called to Christian ministry. It is another one of those divine interruptions that have occurred in my life. Even after being discharged for many, many years, I heard from John Dalen and his family who returned to the States and live in Oregon.

I spent many Sunday afternoons at the base USO (Krabbenlock Service Club). There were a variety of activities. Mostly, my time there was spent playing cards. The center director, Miriam Iverson, arranged activities, including tours for the military personnel. It was through this that I made several visits to Stuttgart, Munich, and various historical sites, including castles and cathedrals, while I was stationed at Neu Ulm. It was on a tour to Munich with Ms. Iverson that I visited my first Chinese restaurant and attempted to learn how to use chop sticks. She, along with so many others, are among the many pleasant memories I have of being in service.

When my tour was over, I still had some furlough time, for which I was paid. I returned to the States aboard the USS Patch, the same ship I had taken to Europe. On both trips, I served as the organist for the chaplaincy program. I had participated on an ongoing basis with the military chaplaincy through my entire military service.

Previously, I mentioned a personnel soldier, Georg Diaz, had aided me in getting appropriate leave so that I could enroll at the University of Geneva and travel behind the Iron Curtain. Diaz was a Cuban immigrant who was drafted into the Army. He had accounting experience, which made him useful to personnel. We became good friends, drinking and travel companions, card players, and champions at the USO Club on base. Yes, we played for money and most often were winners at several card games, including bid whist and canasta. It was here that I picked up extra income. It was also here that I learned many soldiers spent more gambling than their paycheck permitted and needed to borrow money. So, I began to meet their financial need at an appropriate interest rate. I opened a bank account at the local American Express office. I did not leave the army with just the basics.

Reflecting on my time in the military in Germany helped me recall my relationship with George Diaz, an immigrant from Cuba. It was at the army base that I became aware of the diversity of the US Army. Diaz was from Cuba, although he had been drafted from New York. Hugo Ibanez was, I believe, a native of Ecuado, whose family had moved to the United States. He had been drafted. There was a Native American from, I believe, Oklahoma, and many others from places I knew only from world history. The ones mentioned I got to know well although now I cannot recall all the details about them.

In this memoir, I have no hesitation including dark periods from my past. There are many, but each has helped me become a better person and a more compassionate minister of the Gospel of Jesus Christ, which is why there is no reservation for me to tell others.

Looking back over my life, I have no regrets. I am who I am, and became who I became, because of all the experiences over my lifetime. I cannot think of any real changes I would make to my life if it could be lived over, other than probably settling down, getting married, and raising a family. It's possible that I would do so, but I realize that my life has been committed to work since I was a small child, knowing that I had to care for myself with the help of God.

Chapter Five
I Have All that I Need, Except Those Things I Do Not Have...

Returning to the United States in June 1963, I decided to take a trip across country. Greyhound Bus Line had a $99 offer for unlimited travel to all its US destinations. So, I decided to take them up on it by booking a round trip to the West Coast via a northern route and to return to Atlanta via a southern route.

The trip took almost a month. I do not remember all the places I stopped overnight or for a couple of days before pressing on. In the various cities, I would stay at a local YMCA that offered discounts to veterans.

What a summer of unlimited travel! Traveling North from Atlanta, I passed through the Appalachian Mountain region of West Virginia. This had been coal mining country, but the mines had closed. I remember being struck by such deep poverty among white people. Many young men and women had left the coal mines to work in the North at various auto factories and other facilities after both World War II and the Korean War. During the Cold War, many who had gone North lost their good-paying jobs and returned home, but the mines could not accommodate such an influx. Poverty was apparent all along the highways heading north to New York City.

I remember traveling on the famous historic Route 66 in Arizona. I spent several days in Phoenix, arriving there at night with a temperature around 105 degrees! I could not believe how hot it was. People kept telling me that it was dry heat. What I knew was that I had never experienced such heat and could not understand why anyone would want to live in such a hot place. I knew people moved to Arizona because of a variety of health-related issues. Such knowledge did not keep me from wondering, "How could you live in such oppressive heat?"

The westward swing of this trip took me to San Francisco. It was in August 1963, and each day there was heavy overcast skies and a relative low temperature. California did not offer the weather I had expected. I was familiar with the notion that California was a sunny state with little rain. I did not know that there are two distinctive geographical regions in the state. So, visiting beaches where people had on topcoats took me by surprise. I had not packed for cold weather, so my two weeks there were not that enjoyable. My tonsils also gave me problems.

My oldest sister and a brother lived in the Bay Area. My oldest sister lived in San Francisco, and my brother Harry and his family lived in East Palo Alto. My sister and her husband John were involved actively in a variety of things, including owning J & D Liquor Store just outside a navy yard at Hunter's Point and managing parking lots in and around the city, one on Broadway in downtown San Francisco. They also managed a night club in Menlo Park, not far from San Francisco. Both were active in Masonic Lodges. John was a 33-degree mason, a Shriner, and treasurer of his lodge. My sister, Vivian, was most active in the Order of the Eastern Star, holding many positions, including that of Most Ancient Matron, State Loyal Lady, etc.

Vivian became active in the civic affairs of San Francisco. She served as president of CAL-PAC San Francisco Chapter. Along with others, she raised more than two million dollars for the CAL-PAC scholarship fund, an agency of the California Package Store and Tavern Owners Association (CAL-PAC). She wrote numerous articles for various organizations. She received many honors and much recognition for her involvement in the life and activities of San Francisco, including many from the National Council of Negro Women. A "Salute to Vivian Wiley" was held in May 1999 at the Loraine Hansberry Theater in San Francisco with former Mayor Willie L. Brown, Jr., as special guest.

Several times, John Wiley offered to employ me as a business manager if I would give up teaching, then at the University of Detroit, and come to work for him in San Francisco. This happened as he discovered several of his managers were shortchanging him by giving things free to their friends and relatives. Such was easy to do at the night club and the parking lots. In San Francisco, parking is always at a premium. John Wiley had come to trust my judgment, having had many extensive conversations with me following his introducing me to the various businesses and activities in which he was engaged, including that of managing a Masonic housing project. I told him that I was a professional educator and had no real interest in leaving the teaching profession.

Chapter Six
The Gift of Memory

One of the most valuable lessons I have learned is the importance of memory. Some of this has been reflected in the thoughts shared thus far. In responding to the death of someone's loved one, my written response includes a statement like this: "One of the special gifts that each of us has is the gift of memory: memories of both good times and bad times. So, let this God-given gift of good memories sustain your family and you both now and into that time that is yet to be."

As I reflect over these many decades, there are so many good and bad memories. Sometimes, I tell others that there is a negative side to memory. We often tell people we forgive others for their behaviors and actions toward us, but we have real trouble in forgetting. There have been times in my life when I am sure things would have been better between me and someone else had I lost memory of what had created the tension between us. I have come to realize that true forgiveness requires a true reconciliation of the party that has been forgiven, even when forgetfulness is not possible.

How can I forget the health issues that caused a physician to tell my parents that my life expectancy was less than five years? Or, how can I forget that at age twenty-one, I had major surgery for this condition, which meant that I became 1-A for the military draft of that time? I cannot forget much of the negative things people said to me and about me, including family members, simply because I was "different" from others. Yes, even now, some of these memories haunt me with the thought: "Would my life have been different only if...."

Thanks be to God, there are more positive and good memories than negative ones. Moving forward, some of these will be shared, probably along with some of the negative ones. Through it all, my life and connection with the church have sustained and kept me. This I hope to share as this project moves forward. There are lyrics from a previously popular gospel song that went something like this: "I had some good days and some bad days, but my good days outweighed my bad days, so, I won't complain."

Let me back up for a moment and revisit my life in the military, especially that part of it in Germany. There are fond memories of travel to so many places nearby my station. There were Oktoberfests in both Stuttgart and Munich, West Germany. The warm beer, roving bands, and the variety of food—all these things and others made my time with the military go by so quickly. I thought often of how it would have been to remain in Germany in a city like Munich that was so cosmopolitan, even during the Cold War days.

I suppose it was my military service in Germany that created an ongoing interest in the variations of foods. No, it was not from the "chow" served in the dining hall, although it was not as bad as most of us who have served would have others believe. We survived the "SOS" and the K-rations without many, if any, medical complications. In Germany, the food was different, and I learned to appreciate it. Apple strudel became my favorite indulgence at a local pastry shop just outside of the base gate. Traveling in Germany and not speaking German, I learned to order by "picture" or by strange sounding names. This way, I learned what I liked and could order when I was with others and wanted to seem knowledgeable of German food. I discovered early on the appreciation of Wiener Schnitzel—battered and fried veal. I had never given thought to the place and role of veal growing up in the South where fried food is a given. So, it was through German food that I got fascinated with European food and its preparation. It changed my eating habits and desires. From this, as I have traveled, I have sought out local cafes and restaurants just to see what the locals are eating. I have learned to appreciate a variety of foods this way.

One of my more interesting acquaintances was a young recruit whose name, I believe, was Ronald Carney, from Quincey, Massachusetts, who never took a leave and rarely ventured off base doing his time in Germany. His reason: one of his relatives had been killed in Germany during World War II. Although Carney was white, he could find no way to interact with the Germans because of the death of a relative at the height of fighting in Germany during World War II. We spent time together at the Service Club and at a bar located not far from the main entrance of our base.

I made several trips to France, but only one to Paris while in the army. I knew that should I go to Paris first, I probably would not visit any other place nearby, where I was stationed. I took in the usual sites including the Louvre, the Moulin Rouge, with its famous can-can dancers, the Notre Dame Cathedral, and the Arc de Triomphe.

I remember the first time I stood alongside the famous Champs-Elysees, the widest street (boulevard) I had ever seen at that time. Given that I was in Paris more than once, it is somewhat difficult to distinguish now the different times and sights. I know each time there I spent more than a day just touring the halls of the Louvre, never seeing all the exhibits. My trip to Versailles, the Paris Opera House, and walking along the Seine River are fond memories of a young man who was living out a dream and fascination from his recollection of world history. My last trip to Paris occurred sometime in the 1970's, but I do not recollect precisely when except that it was a trip during my teaching days at the University of Detroit.

During my days in Detroit, I met a young man from Sweden who was a master's student in theater at Wayne State University. Per Ohlin was from Stockholm and returned there to start a free theater. I am not sure how it is that I first met Per, but we became friends, I suppose because I had a great interest in the creative arts, and we were about the same age. In any case, once he had returned to Sweden and was ready to open his own theater and production, he invited me to come to the opening.

My trip to Sweden began with booking a flight on Ice Atlantic Airlines through Iceland from Chicago. This was the cheapest way for me to get to Europe. There was a day layover in the capital city of Iceland. Here, I had time to take in the tourist sites. The trip from here took me to Luxembourg, and from Luxembourg, the trip to Rome, Italy was by train. There is so much I could say about the week that I spent in Rome exploring the ruins and places with so much history. What impressed me the most at that time was the amount of poverty just outside the doors of the Vatican. Touring the halls and chambers of the Vatican with all the frescos, gilded windows, statues, and other artistic pieces, then coming outside of its golden archways to find hordes of people, mostly young children, begging for money was somewhat a rude awaking from what had been my mental image of Rome and Vatican City. I met a young Italian boy who spent several days with me, shopping and eating at places where the locals ate, and with few tourists.

The trip to Scandinavia allowed me to visit Belgium, Holland, and Denmark on my way to Sweden. I spent time in each place sightseeing. This was possible given that I had purchased a Euro Rail ticket that allowed unlimited travel and stopover at each stop between Rome and Stockholm. The sights were almost unbelievable. The gardens in each capital city of these countries were in full bloom. I suppose after all these years I remember Copenhagen, Denmark the best. At each major railroad stop, one could find reasonable accommodation, usually a hostel or something similar. I discovered why Denmark is known as the "free love" country. Having grown up in the South in a very conservative environment, seeing how open people lived gave me a new sense of personal freedom and liberty. I do not remember encountering a singular unfriendly person on this trip.

My time in Sweden was spent mostly in Stockholm and the surrounding villages. Per was an ideal host. The museums and theaters were both historic and beautiful. The food proved most impressive. I spent one evening on an island estate where we had crayfish and schnapps. Although

The Gift of Memory

I was familiar with crayfish, I had never eaten them and certainly not in the style served by our hostess. The shells were simply thrown into a big bucket near the huge table. Each "fish" was followed almost immediately by a small drink of Schnapps (vodka). I only remember waking up the next day back in Stockholm in Per's apartment. Although I went there for an opening of a play at a Free Theater, there was a union strike, so I did not get a chance to witness the production directed by Per for which the trip had taken me back to Europe.

Chapter Seven
The Seminary Years

Over the years, I have been asked about my call into Christian ministry. Even now, having written about so much of my life, I cannot in all honesty say when this occurred. In reality, it probably started in my association with the small church of my youth, which came to be my ministry for more than twenty-five years as its senior minister, and now its senior minister emeritus.

Where shall I begin? As I mentioned previously, I heard Dr. Allan K. Knight Chalmers from the School of Theology at Boston University speak at the Fisk University Chapel. The title of his sermon was "Your Signature," and it addressed the quality of one's life and what contributions to society it would make. At that time, I did not know anything about seminaries. I was a chemistry major, and the School of Theology at Boston University practiced and taught, for the most part, what is known as the Social Gospel Movement. None of this explains my movement from math and science to theology. So, I wrestle still with this after all these years. I realize, after many years of being a member of a church and being baptized in it at age nine, it was much later, as an adult, that I really gave my life to Christ.

After the military, I worked at Dobbins Air Force Base, the Electronic Research Center (NASA) in Cambridge, Massachusetts, and the US Post Office. I had taken graduate courses in science education at Atlanta

University (now Clark-Atlanta University). None of this would suggest Christian ministry. Certainly, it should seem somewhat strange given the dark side of my life. Yet, in the fall of 1964, I entered the School of Theology at Boston University in a program leading to a Doctor of Philosophy degree. So, my interest in academics had not changed; its focus had.

Even during my periods of darkness, my appreciation for the church never wavered. I suppose having read the Bible, both the *King James Version* (KJV) and the *Revised Standard Version* (RSV) several times before my teenage years, I realized that much of what I had been taught in my home church was not biblically sound. This weighed on me, and as an educated person, I could help "my people" through what seemed to have dominated the lives of most Negroes. I realized also after being in the public school system that I could see no future in it for me. I had no desire to become a principal or counselor, and I knew after my time at Howard High School that I did not want to spend thirty years of my life chasing Black boys and girls who often had no real interest in education.

Whatever the motivation, when I returned from the military, I knew I would find a career in religion and needed to find myself back in school to do so. I applied only to two programs, both of which would lead to a PhD degree: Boston University School of Theology and the Hartford Theological Foundation in Hartford, Connecticut. My application at both was accepted. The summer of 1963, I visited these two New England cities. Hartford had little real appeal to me. I knew nothing of the Yale Divinity School or the Harvard Divinity School. None of the pastors of my home church had gone to seminary. Only one had held a college degree. I knew of the Interdenominational Center in Atlanta and Chandler School of Theology at Emory University, but neither had an appeal for me. I suppose I still labored under the impression that my education in Atlanta had come to an end. It had not. Boston required certain subjects I had not taken at the undergraduate level, given that I had been a chemistry major. During my year as a physics instructor at Price High School, I enrolled at Georgia State University for several courses.

For admission to Georgia State, I had to appear before an admission council that included administrative officers and faculty. Even in 1963, the public colleges and University of Georgia were still much segregated. I mention this only because at my appearance for admission to Georgia State (GSU), following basic information such as name, date of birth, came the question as a Black person, why I would want to attend GSU when the same courses could be taken at Atlanta University.

Today, when Georgia State University has a sizable enrollment of Black students, such a question would seem absurd. I remember responding as if it happened just last week or so. My response began with stating that my father had worked all his life and paid taxes and that I had worked since around the age of nine and began to pay taxes about the age of fifteen. I said that Georgia State was a public institution supported by all taxpayers of Georgia, and I had a right to attend it. I further stated that the State of Georgia did not have a college or university for Black students in the city of Atlanta. Some of my response had to do with being asked why I did not seek to enroll at Atlanta University. I was admitted to Georgia State and took several courses there, which were offered on the quarter system. At the end of the year, Georgia State sent me a letter telling me that I had been placed on their Dean's List, with Distinction. This letter is among many such notices I have in my collection.

In September 1964, I entered the School of Theology at Boston University as a junior. Part of the orientation process was a series of tests. I believe there were three or four of these. I was assigned to Dr. Herb Stotts, professor of social ethics, for my advisor. He would be the one who would assist me in signing up for classes. One of the first things Dr. Stotts said to me following my entrance into his office was, "Mr. Waters, welcome to the School of Theology. I think that you should start out by just taking the minimum required hours for a full-time student." I reached down, picked up my paperwork from his desk, and went immediately to the Office of the Registrar. There I spoke to Mr. Jones, the registrar, saying: "Mr. Jones, Dr. Stotts could not advise me to cross the street."

This must be set within the context of my admission to the School of Theology with the clear decision that I would be on an accelerated program. That meant at least each semester, I had to take sixteen course hours of work, not just the twelve that would constitute full time status. This decision from the school was based on my various colleges' transcripts, including that from Georgia State. I knew the precise reason Herb Stotts said what he did; I was Black and probably would not do very well at Boston. A similar incident occurred when I went in to see Dr. Douglas, who was to review with me the results of the various tests I had taken during orientation. He began by saying, "Mr. Waters, I am not sure how to interpret these results for you." Dr. Douglas was professor of religious psychology. I said to him, "I believe you should interpret them for me as you would for any other student here at BUST (Boston University School of Theology)."

I had not gone to Boston with any understanding of how real racism was in New England at that time. More could be said about this, and the challenge Black students faced in getting advanced degrees, but more can be found in the pivotal book, *Stony the Road We Trod: African American Biblical Interpretation*, edited by Cain Hope Felder, a Fortress Press publication.

My work at Boston went rather quickly. In May 1967, I received the Bachelor of Sacred Theology degree, *cum laude*, from the School of Theology of Boston University, followed in 1970 with a PhD in biblical studies, Old Testament, from the Graduate School of Boston University. My doctorate was earned in three years, a record at Boston University. Prior to receiving the PhD, the School of Theology asked me to teach an Old Testament course in place of Dr. Harold Beck, who would be on sabbatical.

Now, let me go back and fill in some details of how my life was changed in so many ways while a student at Boston University from 1964–70.

Without a doubt, my studies and time in Boston changed the whole course of my life. Previously, I wrote about my first impression as a beginning student at the historic Boston University School of Theology, or BUST as most of us know it. I entered with a three-quarters full-tuition fellowship provided by this Methodist school. At no time in my six years there was I ever asked or encouraged to become a Methodist or participate in any truly Methodist related activities. Housing and food had to be taken care of as a personal responsibility. To obtain this, I took a position in BUST's media center under the leadership of Dr. Walter Holcomb and worked in the seminary dining hall serving lunch. For housing, I lived in the seminary dormitory at 745 Commonwealth Avenue, a facility that housed all the classrooms, offices, and library for the seminary. In addition, I worked evening as a food server at the university's main dining hall not far from where I lived. At registration time, I worked each semester for the university's Bursar Office, where I collected payment from students at registration. After a session or two with the Bursar Office, the bursar, Mr. Clifton Goodwin, placed me in charge of all the students working for him during registration.

One of my fellow classmates, Ted Bowman, a Mennonite, got a job in a restaurant at the Beacon Street Hotel in Brookline. He told two of his friends, me being one of them, that the hotel was hiring. I got a position as busboy in the Barn, the bar at the hotel, working almost nightly, getting off around 1:00 a.m. This took me from the part time server at BU. This position exposed me to some of the political intrigue of New England. Here, I discovered that many businesses, of necessity, fed and provided other services to political operatives. It was never rare to have Brookline police officers receiving free meals and alcoholic drinks. I learned also of the fellowship and friendship of the regulars at the Barn. The Barn was a relocated barn from New Hampshire that had been dismantled, reassembled, and installed inside of the hotel.

I worked in Brookline from September 1966 to October 1968. At the Barn, I was salaried and was to receive a portion of tips from the bar each night. I discovered rather early on that some nightly bar managers did not share as much as others. I never complained and received praise from the waitresses and bar tenders, and the hotel manager would often compliment me on my punctuality and attention to details. One evening, he asked me to come to his office. He told me that the night manager of their other hotel, the Brookline Inn, had lost his sight from an auto incident. He thought at the time the condition would be temporary. He asked if I would take that position until the man's sight was restored. I had never worked in any capacity at a hotel. He told me that I would make more money and would be there until the gentleman recovered. Being uninformed of the work of a night manager, he had someone show me how to do the work, which included managing bell hops, closing out room tabs each night, and checking clients in and out. In addition, there were several permanent hotel residents whose special needs sometimes had to be taken care of during the evening. After a month or so in the position, it became apparent that the previous night manager had suffered permanent eye damage and would not be able to return to work. Then, I was officially the night manager of the Brookline Motor Inn.

Here is another example of divine intervention. My knowledge of bookkeeping and attention to detail were instrumental in this. Boston and its surroundings attracted visitors for a variety of reasons. As a business hub, many people are in and out of the area frequently. With the various activities around, hotel accommodation was a challenge. As with the bar and regular patrons, so there were regular guests at the hotel. Some of these I got to know rather well. Knowing the schedule of some, when there were times we were about to be overbooked, I would contact them to see if they were coming. If so, I saved them a room. The custom, I suppose, for most hotels is to raise base rates for major events. I did not do this for the regulars. So, it was not that rare that many gave me gifts, especially on special occasions. I discovered also that the Brookline Inn served as a place for some of Boston's "ladies of the evening." It turned out that most of these were female college students supporting their college expenses.

Dr. Holcomb taught me a great deal about media technology for the local church. A part of this was filling requests for material from various New England churches, most of which were Methodist, staffed by graduates of the BU. Seeing that I was a quick and intelligent learner, Dr. Holcomb inquired as to why I was not a Fund for Theology Fellow.

This was a national program designed to prepare Black students for Christian ministry through accredited theological institutions. I told him I had never heard of the program. He informed me that I had to be nominated and that he would submit my name to this organization. The academic requirements were somewhat high; if I remember correctly, one had to have at least a 3.3 grade point average out of a possible 4.0 average. I received this fellowship for the following two years of studies for the Bachelor of Sacred Theology (STB) degree at BU. This degree was awarded with the designation of *cum laude* in 1967.

Arriving at seminary, I had no real understanding of the variety of opportunities for different majors. Given my interest in the Old Testament, as an elective, I chose the Old Testament (the Hebrew Bible). In my beginning class of Hebrew, taught by Dr. H. Neil Richardson, there were about twelve of us. Within a few weeks, six of us remained. Dr. Richardson became my advisor. One of the most interesting required courses was Introduction to Old Testament History by Dr. Harold Beck, who had a reputation as both an inspiring teacher and profound preacher.

I lived at 745 Commonwealth Avenue for four of my years in Boston. I remained in Boston even during the summer months. Due to a positive relationship with Ms. Dorothy Lord, secretary to the dean of the School of Theology, Dr. Walter Muelder, this became possible. Boston was and still is one of the most expensive American cities in which to live. During summer months, I worked at various places, including the Electronic Research Center (NASA) in Cambridge. (This was later moved to Houston, Texas.) During the Christmas breaks each year, I worked at the main US Post Office in Boston. These positions were available to me as a US veteran. One summer, I went to work in the evening for a professional cleaning company. All of this I relate simply to say that education was so important to me that I sought what I thought was the best. And my studies did not suffer given my work schedule. In hindsight, my grade point average may have been a bit higher had I not worked, but I did not do badly even with a work schedule. I learned the importance of what is now termed "time management."

Utilizing Boston University membership in a consortium of divinity schools, I was able to take courses at any locally accredited divinity school. This cross-registration process was open only to those students with a certain grade point average and for certain offerings. Taking advantage of this program, I took several Old Testament courses at the Harvard University Divinity School. Harvard had a distinguished faculty that included Dr. G. Earnest Wright, Dr. Thorkild Jacobsen, and others. Dr. Wright is still a highly respected Old Testament scholar and Dr. Jacobsen a noted Assyriology scholar. Both these men were instrumental in my doctoral studies at Boston. Of the two, perhaps the late G. Earnest Wright is the better known, although Dr. Jacobsen's work in the field of ancient intellectual pursuits is still referenced by so many modern historians and scholars of antiquity.

My degree in Hebrew Bible (Old Testament) required proficiency in numerous ancient languages, including Akkadian, Ugaritics, and Greek. Given that much of Old Testament scholarship had been done by German scholars, German was also a major requirement. To receive the degree, an examination was required in both Greek and German. There were few students in the language program for the STB degree, and even fewer for the PhD program administered by the Graduate School of Arts and Sciences at Boston. All advance Greek classes were taught through the faculty of School of Arts and Sciences. Several of these had me as the only student! All the other ancient languages were taken under the supervision of Dr. Richardson. I employed the mentoring of a well-known German teacher in the Boston area for the study of German. German is not one of the easiest languages to learn for a variety of reasons. Fortunately, having lived in Germany, I had some familiarity with the language and its construction, so the study went relatively well. It would seem that language study for me would have been easy given I began with Latin and French in high school and continued French for two years in college. It was not, and even now, I wonder, sometimes, how it was I was able to complete the seven languages requirements for the degree at Boston. This too, I credit with divine intervention.

It may seem strange that my doctoral work at Boston University was completed in three years. Traditional PhD programs in general take five to eight years. However, given the modern age with online courses, this has changed. Many who were in graduate school with me broke up their course studies, dissertation preparation, and other matters related to completing this academic degree. Since Boston had given me a fellowship for the PhD program, I was receiving support from the GI Bill, and I was continuously working while at Boston, I had no need to suspend my pursuit of that which I had set out to accomplish.

Dr. H. Neil Richardson was my adviser throughout almost all my days at BUST and Dr. Harold Beck became my second reader for my doctoral dissertation. In reality, Dr. Beck was to be my PhD advisor, but his sabbatical and a period of illness had Dr. Richardson to become such. What occurred here was that the focus of my dissertation project as agreed to by Dr. Beck was changed by Dr. Richardson. I had sense enough to know not to challenge Dr. Richardson's decision and authority. My final dissertation topic was "The Political Development and Significance of the Shepherd-King Symbol in the Ancient Near East and in the Old Testament."

The research work for the dissertation proved to be an extension of some of the material that I worked on with Dr. Richardson. Additional bibliographical work took me often to the Harvard Divinity School Library, and I used the acquisition of materials from other collections through a library loan relationship Boston had with other libraries. Having mastered Kate Turabian's *A Manual for Writers of Term Papers, Theses, and Dissertations,* in additional to being well disciplined in all aspects of life, my dissertation completion went rather quickly. From my early days at BUST, I discovered the importance of a detailed outline prior to writing a paper.

Adhering rigidly to the outline for the dissertation made the research and writing seem rather straight forward. With typing skills, I rented an IBM Selectric™ typewriter and acquired the necessary Hebraic module that would be required for the manuscript. As I wrote, the material was passed on for review to my roommate, Michael Bille, an English major at Boston College. When the entire manuscript had been completed, another friend, Richard Roebuck, was asked to read it for typical errors, grammatical issues, etc. Once all this had been accomplished, the finished manuscript was given to one of my college friends, Fletcher Dalton, who was a college book editor for a publishing company in Boston. Fletcher had been a music major at Fisk but, as with so many of us, had found a position in another area.

Once all this had been done, the final manuscript was given to Dr. Richardson. He told me it needed to receive approval from the second reader, Dr. Beck, prior to his reading and approval. So, I made an appointment to see Professor Beck and present him with the final manuscript. Dr. Beck said, "Brother Waters, can you read Egyptian Hieroglyphics?"

My response was "No."

He then said: "Before I read your dissertation, you will have to be able to read Egyptian Hieroglyphics."

I was somewhat crushed since such an idea had never been asked of me before or even suggested. After leaving his office and calming down, I thought "I have not put in all this time and effort to just walk away in disgust at a last-minute requirement that appeared nowhere in writing for my work."

So, I went to the BU Library and found a copy of Gordon's Ancient Egyptian grammar text. As it turned out, Hieroglyphics is a pictorial writing style and the key is knowing the meaning of each symbol. I knew the term as well as the significance of the Rosetta Stone and its place in understanding writings on the pyramids, but had not given that much thought as to why I should have a basic understanding of this. Then, it dawned on me that the shepherd symbol, of which was the basic component of my dissertation, was most significant in Ancient Egypt. It made perfect sense that I understood this. So, I made an appointment with Professor Beck where I demonstrated my reading ability of

The Son of My Father

Pyramid writing. He then accepted my dissertation manuscript and said he would inform me when he had finished reading it.

About a month later, I was back in Dr. Beck's office, where he informed me that there was a real problem with some of my understanding of Hebrew verb form and that such corrections had to be made before he signed off on it. Again, anger arose in me. Now, in much hindsight, I, too, have had to explain to others the sense of time in biblical Hebrew. I knew this from all the Hebrew language studies I had done. It was simple to resort to my understanding of time from my study of English and other languages. I made the changes but did not do the retyping myself. I had become a friend of the secretary of the Department of Practical Theology (Field Study). When sharing with her my frustration, she said she would do the retyping without charge, which she did. With this accomplished, the dissertation manuscript was once again given to Dr. Beck. Within a month, he had read it and approved it. This was then taken to Dr. Richardson who said that if Dr. Beck had approved it there was no reason for him to read it and immediately signed off on it. There was only one more hurdle to encounter, the Defense of the Dissertation. Dr. Richardson set this in motion.

The title of the dissertation, written previously, was relatively long, but this is in keeping with many dissertations' titles. What the finished product indicates is that the writer is now an expert in a very narrow field of study. It's so interesting that the more I became educated, the more I realized how little I knew. That supports my basic belief that "education begins at birth and ends at death; therefore, we should always be learning." This, then, is the basic premise of my doctoral dissertation. Here is a brief summary of my findings :

> The general term in the Ancient Near East for a shepherd is based on an Akkadian root, *reum*. The second rarely used Semitic term denoting "shepherd" is *nqd*. The cognates are based on a Sumerian root, *NSGAD*. The term has specialized meaning of "chief of the shepherds.

The data gathered support the following conclusions about Mesopotamian political structures: kingship emerged out of the council of elders as a possible solution to the socio-economic problems of the community; the descriptive symbol which evolved for the role of the king was that of the shepherd; the politico-military significance of this symbolism was retained from the earliest periods down through the fall of the Babylonian-Assyrian Empire; and, the authority which was associated with the symbolism was projected into the cosmos.

The political structures of ancient Egypt were similar to those of Mesopotamia. The pharaoh, however, is the best example of what was implied politically by the shepherd symbol.

The historical development of the symbol of the king as shepherd indicates that the shepherd-king symbol was used in cultures in which domestic animals were essential to the economy; the shepherd was selected as a prototype for the king because of his responsibility and relationship to his flock; and the primary significance of the symbol was its politico-military overtones.

The study concludes that wherever the shepherd-king symbolism emerged the related political structures was autocratic. It is concluded that Israel's political structure was analogous to the role of the shepherd to his flock. Under David, and perfected under Solomon, the autocratic rule in Israel was realized. The symbol used most often in Israel to refer to her kings, especially in the prophetic tradition, was that of the shepherd. It was the autocratic policies of the kings of Israel which led the nation into the political disaster which resulted in the fall of both kingdoms.

The data gathered for this study indicate several possibilities for farther studies in the areas of: Ancient Near Eastern symbolism as well as Old Testament symbolism; the use of the shepherd symbol in the New Testament; and the vestiges of the "shepherd as leader symbol" in contemporary religious circles.

Chapter Eight
Whom God Calls, He Qualifies...

Writing from this distance makes it necessary from time to time to break a trend of thought. Such comes now. I had gone to Boston with the clear intention of studying for the PhD degree. I had no connection with a church there, although each Sunday, I visited one of the many historic churches in the area. One Sunday, I visited the well-known Peoples Baptist Church in Roxbury, a Black church. Given the distance from campus, it was more convenient to visit other churches. There were no Black congregations near BU. At the time, the late Howard Thurman was dean of chapel at Boston. I found his messages to be lacking in whatever it was I was seeking.

There are so many historic churches in Boston. I believe that I visited all those along Boylston Street at least one or more times. Some I worshiped in on Sundays. The Protestant church nearest the campus had been pastored by Cotton Mather. One of his descendants, Richard, was a classmate. I believe Richard was a Christian scientist and became a missionary. I read of his passing and recalled that we shared several classes together. From time to time, I visited Peoples' Baptist Church in Roxbury, pastured by the late Rev. Richard Owens. It was the Park Street Church on Beacon Hill where I went most often until I became associated with the Ebenezer Baptist Church in the South End of Boston.

Park Street Church, an American Baptist Church, was pastored by the late Rev. Dr. Harold Ockenga, a founding president of Fuller Theological Seminary in California. He was bi-vocational, serving both the church and seminary. The Park Street Church had a history of great, involved pastors, including William Lloyd Garrison, who was much involved in the antislavery movement. I am not sure now how I first heard of Park Street, but I do know that Dr. Ockenga was well regarded as a great preacher. He was a Neo-Evangelistic believer. On most Sundays, the sanctuary was packed with noted scientists and scholars. I came to know some of them and wondered why they would worship at Park Street. I was informed that "most of their time was spent on speculative thought, but on Sundays, they were told what to believe." Trained as a chemist, I understood that both science and religion was in the pursuit of the truth. I would take the "T" to Park Street and often return home on Commonwealth Avenue by walking. In Boston, I discovered the great pleasure in walking. Boston is known for its gardens, paths, and fountains and is one of the great walking cities of the world. Over the years, each time I have returned, I have found myself walking through the Boston Commons.

On one cold Saturday morning in January 1965, I got a call from the Reverend Dr. William Ravenell, Sr., pastor of Boston's Ebenezer Baptist Church in the South End on the edge of Roxbury. Dr. Ravenell said he had been informed that I was Baptist, and he was interested in talking with me about becoming his youth minister. This was interesting, given that I had not at that time visited his church, had not been ordained, and had never expressed interest in serving as a youth minister. I had gone to Boston with the clear intent of pursuing an academic career. I think, at that time, I had visited only one Black church in Boston—People's Baptist Church, which was not located that far from Ebenezer. The position of youth ministry was new to me. My home church never had one, although there were several youths attending there.

After meeting with Dr. Ravenell, I agreed to work with the youth of Ebenezer. It turned out that there were few of them, and there was a woman in charge who seemed lost in how youth thought and functioned.

There were maybe ten or twelve youth in the youth group. Currently, I do not recall the youth group leader's name. In addition to working with the youth, Dr. Ravenell asked me to teach the youth Sunday school class. At no point did he ever discuss any compensation for my service, and I did not ask for any. In the church where I had grown up, only the pastor received any compensation. Many times, to get to Ebenezer during my first year there, I walked from Commonwealth Avenue. I took about thirty minutes to do so. I was never bothered by this, since taking transit from BU there took almost as long.

Soon after becoming the youth minister, I met with the interested youth and began by asking, "What are your interests?" No one said anything. The female leader then told me that they would never tell her anything, which is why she planned all their activities. I told her this was not my approach. So, I said to them, "We will sit here until you begin to tell me some of your interests." These were teenagers, all in school. When they saw I was serious and provided no recommendation for activities, they began to speak. Out of this conversation, I learned that some were interested in careers in science and mathematics, some had issues with their parents, some had issues with the quality of their education, etc. Out of this discussion came the idea to sponsor a church science fair for teenagers. The young people were asked to invite their friends to participate.

The initial response to inviting kids from outside Ebenezer to Ebenezer did not sit well with some of its members. Many members thought Ebenezer to be the church for the elite and sophisticated Black people. There were a number of professionals, including politicians, teachers, and doctors. Dr. Ravenell had an earned doctorate and had been professor of elocution at North Carolina State prior to becoming pastor of Ebenezer. The youth were asked to invite their friends to a Saturday Open House. To my surprise, I was informed that Ebenezer did not want kids to come from the neighborhood or from homes whose parents they did not know. I knew then that my time at Ebenezer would challenge me, given that I was from one of those home they were talking about. Even today, we have to remind Black people that we, too, practice a class system. Nevertheless, my position prevailed, and we had a Science Fair with about thirty kids from around Boston. From my association at BUST, guidance counselors were brought to several meetings to help the youth deal with issues they faced. The youth group began to grow. Similar results took place in the Sunday school. The standard materials that had been used for them were discarded. Instead, we made use of my association with the media center at BUST. More of this material was geared for youth with pictures of Black people rather than a preponderance of images of white people. Eventually, Dr. Ravenell asked me to become superintendent of the Sunday school.

One of the first people Dr. Ravenell introduced to me was Mrs. Mary Luck, president of the Progressive Club. Mrs. Luck informed me that the Progressive Group always raised the most money for the church and that she had been its president for fifty-nine years. I remember saying to her, "Mrs. Luck, do you have any idea how much could have been raised over the years if there had been others who served as president of the Progressive Club?" From that point on, it was most rare that Mrs. Luck spoke to me, although she was very active in the life of Ebenezer.

It became my custom to attend Sunday school at Ebenezer and occasionally remain for Sunday worship, which began at 10:30 a.m. As a student who worked, I had reasons to leave to catch up with various assignments or sometime just to leave the city. In those days, I would travel to New York, where I had several friends. Sometimes I would fly, in those days for around thirty-five dollars. Sometimes I would take the train or bus. My first classes were on Tuesdays. Previously, I mentioned both Freddie Morgan and George Diaz who lived there, George in Manhattan's Greenwich Village and Freddie in Brooklyn. Once in New York, I stayed with one of them at no cost and often had to buy no food. Those were some good ole days to say the least. But, back to Dr. Ravenell, who said to me one Sunday, "Brother Waters you could wear white shirts on Sundays." Being a working student, white shirts were not something to which I paid much attention. Nevertheless, given that it was Ebenezer, I began to wear white shirts each Sunday.

One Sunday, after Sunday school, Dr. Ravenell asked if I wanted to sit in the pulpit. I told him no. He then said, "You know you should remain at church each Sunday because it would make a good impression on our young people." I began to do this. At that time, Reverend Ravenell had one ministerial associate, Reverend Smith. Each Sunday, Reverend Smith prayed, almost word for word, the same prayer. Ebenezer had Bible study on Friday evenings. Here, too, Reverend Smith prayed the same prayer. The only times Reverend Ravenell allowed him to preach was at the Friday Bible study. It was clear that he was not seminary trained and did not seek to improve his status in ministry.

One Sunday morning, following Sunday school, Dr. Ravenell came to me saying that he was ill and was going home. He said, "You will give the sermon today." Worship began at 10:30 at Ebenezer, so he must have said that to me around 10:00 a.m. The only sermon I had ever given was at my home church in 1963 which was required to be licensed as a Christian minister, which was an admission requirement at Boston University School of Theology. Dr. Ravenell left and I sat a few minutes in his office thinking of what to preach. I do not remember what it was, but I do remember that I rambled on and on for what seemed to be an hour. I had made no outline or notes, so it all came from my memory. No one walked out and no one fell asleep, as far as I know. From this experience, when given the opportunity to preach, I used an outline. This, for me, took too much time, so I began using a twenty-minute manuscript. These "sermons" could last about a half hour. I do not remember the pastor ever using an outline or manuscript in my Atlanta home church.

Dr. Ravenell took me under his wing by inviting me to go with him to various ministerial meetings in the Boston area. Ebenezer was an American Baptist congregation with a loose affiliation with the Progressive National Baptist Convention. Traveling with Dr. Ravenell gained me membership in a variety of local associations, including the Massachusetts Baptist Convention. Boston, being the capitol city, and the former home of Roger Williams, the founder of the Baptist Church in America, had several prominent Baptist Churches and preachers, mostly white.

One Sunday following church, Dr. Ravenell asked me to come visit him at his home in Dorchester. This I did the following week, having no idea why he invited me to his home rather than meeting with him in his office at Ebenezer. I was in for a surprise in many ways.

At his home, Dr. Ravenell asked me to allow him to ordain me. He said although he had pastored the church for thirty-seven years, he had never ordained anyone. To say I was taken by surprise on several levels would be stating it mildly. I told him I was not a member of Ebenezer and that it was my belief that a person should be ordained at his home church. I agreed to speak to the Rev. L. C. Robinson, pastor of Solid Rock in Atlanta, which I did via telephone. He had no problem with this. I asked if he would come to Boston for the ordination. He said he could not afford to do so but that I had his blessing. This I reported back to Dr. Ravenell. That following Sunday, I joined Ebenezer and Dr. Ravenell announced to the church that he was setting in motion the procedure for my ordination at Ebenezer.

The ordination was set for the second Sunday of May 1967 (Mother's Day). This would be the same year and month the School of Theology at Boston University awarded me the STB degree *cum laude*. The procedure for the ordination was set by the Boston West-South Association of the American Baptist Churches of America. The written procedures were provided to me. As is the custom with Baptists, an ordination council is called by the secretary of the association with the assistance of the pastor of the ordinand.

I prepared for the ordination council with guidance from Dr. Ravenell. There were two sessions, both held at the First Baptist Church of Brookline. The council voted, unanimously, to recommend that Ebenezer Church proceed with the ordination without reservation. (Sometimes it is necessary to explain to others how the Baptist Church conducts its affairs. And it seems that each has its own variation on almost any ritual or procedure, and ordination to the Christian ministry is no exception.) Dr. Ravenell presented the recommendation to the congregation, which voted its acceptance. With this done, Dr. Ravenell shared with me an ordination worship service.

I was told that I could invite whomever I pleased to participate. I asked about the sermon. He said I was free to invite whomever I wanted. One of the great preachers at Boston University was Dr. Harold Beck, my Old Testament professor. I asked him to give the sermon, and he immediately accepted the invitation. As a member of the Seminary Singers, I asked the director, Dr. Max Miller, to allow them to sing. Dr. Miller was also the university organist. One of my classmates, Dr. Calvin Morris, a Seminary Singers soloist, was asked to perform a specific selection, which he agreed to do. All of this was set in motion more than a month in advance.

Each component was shared with and approved by Dr. Ravenell. Within a couple of weeks before the ordination was to take place, Dr. Ravenell died. Indeed, I was heartbroken for this senior pastor who had gone out of his way to be so helpful to me. He provided a model of Christian ministry for me, which, even after all these years, I respect: You can be educated and serve a Black Baptist congregation without regrets of formal theological education.

The ordination was a good occasion, even with the Ebenezer family mourning the loss of its senior pastor. The church called one of BU's doctoral students, the Rev. Charles Brown, to serve as interim pastor, which he did for a year or so. Although I had never really functioned in a pastoral role, Rev. and Mrs. Brown assumed that I would seek to pastor Ebenezer, and I discovered early on the vicious competitiveness of those seeking a pulpit. I had not gone to Boston to pastor and gave no thought as to who would follow Dr. Ravenell. It was not Reverend Brown. The church called the Rev. Raphe Taylor from Connecticut, and my relationship with the church remained intact under his leadership.

Meanwhile, upon completing the STB degree, I was admitted to the PhD program at the Graduate School of Arts and Sciences at Boston. I had applied to three doctoral programs, but I remained at Boston since I had been admitted to its School of Theology with the understanding that I would pursue an academic degree to teach. In addition, the school awarded me a fellowship for doctoral studies.

Chapter Nine
You Should Not Judge a Book By...

Such a familiar quotation as, "You should not judge a book by its cover," is often quoted in personality discussions. To a degree, there is some logic to it. Although the cover may not indicate the value and worth of the book's content, its title should do so. This is sited in retrospect to my initial days as a student at the School of Theology at Boston University. I arrived as an older, Black student who had been admitted with a science degree.

My future had been planned with extreme care. I would teach in some graduate school. What I had not given serious thought to was serving the church in any capacity other than a member. This changed when the senior pastor of the Myrtle Street Baptist Church, West Newton, Mass., decided to resign and take a position at the Andover Newton School of Theology. I do not remember how it was that the pastoral search committee of the church thought it should seek an interim and allow itself time to find a full-time senior pastor.

While studying for the degree at Boston in 1968, I received a call from the Myrtle Baptist Church, asking me to interview for its interim pastor position. I was not looking for such a position, but my relationship with the Ebenezer Baptist Church had me devoted to the degree that I simply agreed to come for the interview. The interview was most interesting.

I was informed about the history of the church. Myrtle Baptist was organized in 1874, its founding membership being comprised of Negroes in the area as well as those coming from the South in search of better living conditions. This took place soon after the Civil War had ended, and the era of Reconstruction were underway. This was not an especially good time for Black people anywhere in America. Over the years, Myrtle grew and attracted many professionals. I was told at the interview that all the adults were college educated and their children were destined to go to college.

I do not recall the size of the Search Committee, which included Mrs. Lillie Jefferson, who was secretary of the church and functioned, for the most part, as its administrator. She was married to Matt Jefferson, who was a member of the city council. One of the members of the church served as superintendent of the public school system. There were various faculty members, including Dr. Orlando Lightfoot, a psychiatrist from Harvard University who had been a classmate of mine at Fisk University.

After a series of rather personal questions, I said to the committee, "Let me suggest to you the type of questions you should be asking." My suggestions focused on educational qualification, commitment to raising the spiritual awareness of members, building relationships beyond the membership, etc. Much of this came from my relationship with Reverend Ravenell from Ebenezer. I left the meeting certain that I would not hear from them again.

Within a week or so, I got a call from Mrs. Jefferson, asking if I would accept their interim appointment. I was surprised to say the least. I had never served in the capacity of presiding minister of a church and had only served in the youth ministry at Ebenezer. Even now, I remind others that I did not attend seminary to become the pastor of a church. I accepted the offer and served there as its interim pastor until I became an adjunct instructor of Old Testament at Boston University School of Theology.

Serving the Myrtle Church challenged me in many ways, positive and negative. The first such experience occurred on the first Sunday that

I served Myrtle Baptist. I arrived and visited several of the Sunday school classes, refusing to say anything in them. I took mental notes. The Sunday worship was posted for 11:00 a.m., but the musician for the church had not arrived. I waited in the pastor's study to be told by the chairman of the deacon board that worship was ready to begin. That happened around 11:20! Needless to say, this bothered me to no end given my habit of punctuality learned from my father.

It was my task to give the call to worship. There were those present who did not stand for the call to worship, which was an experience new to me. So, I stopped and said to the congregation, "There are two groups of us here today, those who have come to worship and those who have come to watch. We will issue the call to worship again, and those who have come to worship will stand and we will begin our worship together."

At the time of the ministerial comments, I announced "that beginning with the following Sunday, we could do one of two things: change the signage outside announcing the time of worship to "around" or "about" 11:00 a.m. or begin on time. We will begin on time," I said, "whether the musician is present or not. Given that the announcements are printed in the bulletin, they will not be read during the service. Should anyone need them read, give me a call Sunday afternoon and I will read them to you." I never received such a call.

Reading the church membership profile, I discovered that several professionals were not sharing their careers and educational training with the Myrtle Street Family. One such member was an associate superintendent of the school system, and several worked in the fields of accounting and bookkeeping. I asked why they had such limited participation at the church. Their response was not that unusual in the Baptist church; they had not been asked. The superintendent was asked to share with the Sunday school and those in the field of accounting and bookkeeping to share with the Budget Committee. Helping others understand the reason for the request made the transitioning easier.

When asked how I could know these members could be trusted, my response was "divine intervention." In general, I have been rather good at judging character upon first impressions and conversation. As a survivor of such, I have learned to depend on my reflexive thought process.

For many Black Baptists, we are told that the two places in the church where "all hell" can break out are the music ministry and the deacon's board. I found this to be true in the several congregations I had the pleasure to serve. As summer approached during my interim service in West Newton, I was told the choir would not sing during the summer and the worship would begin earlier due to the high humidity in the area. That was fine with me. I asked anyone interested in singing in a summer choir to let me know. I contacted Fletcher Dalton, who was a music major at Fisk, and asked him to work with us during the summer. He did and there was a marked improvement in our music ministry. At neither of my churches were there any serious issues with the deacons except introducing them to the Deacon Family Ministry program

Soon after coming to Myrtle, one of the young female members, a teacher in a local public school, asked if she could meet with me. She had been married for a bit more than a year. According to her, she prepared a lunch for her husband every day, who then left home to go to work. The problem was that he had lost his job several months before. Now unemployed, he left their house and spent every day at his mother's home. She said she had lost confidence in him and wanted to know if it would be a sin to divorce him. Discussing this with her, I said, "None of us are perfect and we all make mistakes. So, if it is your desire to file for a divorce do so." She took my advice and later told me how pleased she now was.

As my work at Myrtle moved forward, Dr. Harold Beck at Boston University took a sabbatical. At the suggestion and recommendation of Dr. Richardson, my primary advisor and dean of the school, asked me to serve as an adjunct in the Introduction of the Old Testament class during the semester as Dr. Beck would be out of the country. Discussing the offer and request, I told the dean that to leave Myrtle to teach at the STH would be a reduction in income. Dean Muedler pointed out that the reason I was in Boston was to become a teacher. He was right, so I resigned my position at the church.

When I was ordained at Ebenezer in 1967, one of its gifts was a ministerial robe and a traveling case. I took both with me to Myrtle and stored them there. The previous pastor had not moved all his things, but when he did he also took my traveling bag. Contacting him about it, Rev. O'Neal denied ever seeing it and told me that I had to be mistaken. This made me aware that there are lying preachers. Certainly, in the days of the 21st century, such is evident.

The congregation was Baptist, associated with the American Baptist Convention. During my interim, the John A Volpe was governor of Massachusetts, and he served in this capacity from 1963–65. Behind the church was a major interstate with a small parcel of land. The Howard Johnson corporation sought to establish one of its café locations there on the major thoroughfare. With the assistance of one of the local politicians of the church, we held several meetings with the governor. He agreed to have the state cede the track to the church, where a playground was established. This helped me fashion some principles for the pastoral ministry that would prove helpful in other endeavors.

It would seem that as soon as I entered the PhD program I started thinking about where I would find a teaching position. I am not sure when I was introduced to *The Chronicle of Higher Education*, but I was a subscriber even when I served as an interim at the Fellowship Missionary Baptist Church in Minnesota. Along the way, I knew my focus would be becoming an educator rather than a teacher. At Boston, I had no female instructors and there was one Black instructor, Dr. Preston Williams, in ethics, I believe, but I did not take any of his course offerings.

I mentioned previously my membership in the Society of Biblical Studies. In the fall of 1968, it held its annual convention in Boston. At each of its annual meetings, there was always an opportunity for faculty recruiters to meet prospects. There, I met the chairman of the Religion and Philosophy Department of the University of Detroit, a Jesuit school. I was invited out to Detroit and was offered the position of assistant professor of religious studies with the understanding that I would receive my degree in May of 1970. The visit to the University of Detroit was eye-opening in many ways.

The University of Detroit was not the only school for which I interviewed and visited; I was also interested in the Interdenominational Theological Center (ITC) in Atlanta and the Wesley Theological School in Washington, D.C. Each offered me a faculty position as an assistant professor. Wesley was determined to hire me, so its president, Dr. Harold DeWolf, paid me a visit one Sunday while I served the Myrtle Church. I applied also to Rice University in Texas. I gave very serious thought to each offer and decided that I did not wish to teach at a seminary-oriented institution. In those days, Methodist institutions had its faculty sign pledge cards to abstain from the use of tobacco and alcohol.

Chapter Ten
Blessed Assurance

"Wherefore thou art no more a servant, but a son…" (Gal. 4:7).

In May 1970, the Graduate School of Arts and Science awarded me the PhD degree in biblical studies (Hebrew Bible). The following August, I relocated to Detroit to become an assistant professor of theology at the University of Detroit, where I remained for six years, obtaining tenure and the status of associate professor and director of the Center for Black Studies. My time in Detroit came during a period when the auto industry was downsizing and much unrest existed in several areas.

It was in Detroit where I discovered the vast difference in a Catholic and a Jesuit school. Jesuits do not take a vow of poverty and chastity. Nearby was a college for women run by nuns, and several of the priests at the university dated the sisters of the nearby college. All the priests dressed well, including Father Malcom Carron, S. J., the president. Several belonged to a nearby country club. On my initial visit to the university, arriving on a Sunday, I was asked if I would like something to drink. I thought it would be water, coffee, or tea, but instead I was taken to a room that would seem to put any of the local bars to shame given its wide collection. Detroit turned out to be a city where you could acquire almost anything any day of the week. There is some advantage to living in such a place. I became a tenured faculty member at the University of Detroit and chair of its Center for Black Studies. I remained there for six years, leaving to return home to Atlanta where my mother had also returned after living a brief time in the San Francisco, Calif., area.

As a faculty member with a PhD degree at the University of Detroit, I had to offer at least one graduate course per semester. Most of these courses were offered in the evening. The university offered a master's degree in religious studies. Given its diverse faculty in the department, the courses covered a wide variety of areas, including Judaism. As a teaching Catholic institution, it offered classes for Catholic seminarians who were destined for the priesthood. It also provided courses for students of Marygrove College, an all-girls school run exclusively by nuns.

Detroit provided opportunities for me to grow in many areas. Long term friendships developed both at the university and beyond. The first wedding at which I was the best man occurred there at the People's Community Church. The Rev. Oliver White, who was a student of mine and who had become a friend, asked me to be his best man. I do not recall why I did not ask him about a relative or other close friend. Oliver, although a student, was close in age to me. He served as a musician at a nearby Baptist Church. As a native of Detroit, he was instrumental in me getting to know the city much better. Although there were a number of Black students at U of D, the majority was white and Catholic.

Some Sundays, I visited Hartford Memorial Church, pastored by one of my Fisk University classmates, Rev. Charles Adams. True to Black Baptist traditions, the services were quite long. Eventually, Hartford moved from Detroit to Southfield, Mich., purchasing what had been a white Baptist church. With a much larger facility, Hartford added additional programs, including a school, a restaurant, and a day care. My visits here decreased, given the distance to drive from where I lived.

One of my favorite spots in Detroit is Belle Isle, where there is an aquarium and a mini zoo. One Sunday, while there, I met a young lady who was a nursing student at Wayne State University. Barbara Davis was a native of Detroit, a model, hair stylist, and jazz musician.

We dated for most of my time in Detroit and many thought that we would get married. Barbara became someone with whom I could share much of my life. One evening, I took her to one of the better-known restaurants near Belle Isle. As we were leaving and waiting for my car to be brought around by a valet, a white man walked up to me, handed me his car keys, and said, "bring my car around." This was not the first time racism in Detroit was made so apparent to me. I was dressed well, in a tailored suit and tailored topcoat trimmed in fur, but I was Black, so I had to be an employee at this expensive restaurant. I assured the man that, as he wanted his car, mine was being brought around. It was a relatively new Mercury Cougar, black trimmed in red.

I arrived in Detroit at the time the country was going through the aftereffects of race riots following the assassination of the Rev. Dr. Martin Luther King, Jr. I had witnessed the effect of this in Boston, when so many white people came into the South End and Roxbury with their help and assistance. The tension in Detroit was somewhat different. The automotive driven economy was in a free fall; layoffs and reduced salary were beginning to be common. Detroit was a union driven city where Poles and Blacks belonged to different unions all affiliated with the AFL (American Federation of Labor). With job openings in short supply, the Poles and Blacks competed for the same jobs. At the same time, many Blacks who worked had begun to move into predominantly white neighborhoods. Detroit had experienced a similar situation during the Great Depression, when Blacks migrated from the south seeking better living conditions, and after World II, when returning Black soldiers began to insist on equality at all levels.

I could spend some time discussing how I found out about Detroit's racial history, including how the Catholic Church forced those Blacks seeking better education for their children than the public schools provided to convert to Catholicism. This is how the Davis children, the family of which I spoke earlier, had its three children educated—each finishing the parochial schools and then going to Wayne State University.

At the University of Detroit, the faculty at the Center for Black Studies was in turmoil as to its direction. There was a director, several full-time members, and several members who were full time in other departments of the university. For some reason, again divine intervention, the academic dean asked me if I would be interested in assuming the directorship and bring some sense of stability to it. At this point, I had never chaired any committee anywhere. I suppose they thought given my reputation in the Department of Religious Studies as a no-nonsense member and being Black with a PhD that I would be a good fit. As an established, tenured faculty member, my relationship as an associate professor of religious studies could bring something that would make a difference in its Black Studies Department.

The center's offices were in a high rise just across the street from the main campus of the university. It had its own budget. The university had guidelines for departmental procedures and standards. One thing that was clear to me was if I were to lead this department, I should have at least some course offerings in it. To do this, I spent much time reading about the history of the Black Church in America. I was familiar with some of this from my time spent in the Black Library Collection as a student at Fisk University.

Out of my concern, I developed a course: The History of the Black Church, which became a popular offering. One of the class assignments was for the student to trace the history of his or her home church. Since most of the students were from Detroit, the assignment would not require travel. To no surprise, students discovered things about their home churches they never knew. Detroit has several historic Black churches of various denominations. There were several Muslim students and non-affiliated students. The Muslims wrote about their mosque and the non-affiliated chose another topic.

As an aside, there have been Black churches in America even before the Civil War—churches located in both North and South. Perhaps the better-known histories are that of the American Methodist Episcopal Church (AME), founded by Richard Allen, and Baptist churches. Even today, the majority of Black Christians hold membership in these denominations.

My work at the University of Detroit allowed many positive things to occur in my life—working as the director of the Center for Black Studies and gaining an interest in the AAUP, which led to an involvement in organizing a campus chapter union to address many of the concerns of some faculty about various issues, including salaries, class size, and working conditions. This led me to a number of meetings with the National Labor Relations Board. Eventually, the union effort failed, but the experience proved helpful in many ways. I was also president of the AAUP chapter at the university.

My involvement with labor relations at the university led me to study the union movement and its relationship to Black workers. A course developed from this study. As a Black administrator, I became involved with a national group of Black administrators and eventually presented a paper at one of its annual meetings at the University of Washington in Seattle, Washington. My years at the University of Detroit helped me in so many ways to become that professional educator of which I dreamed growing up in Atlanta. Then the goal was to become a science teacher.

My six years in Detroit came as the city experienced major changes in so many ways. The auto industry was in decline, inflation was quite high, and Black academics were being recruited by major white institutions of higher learning all over the county. I suppose I became restless and desired to relocate. This occurred at the same time my mother decided to return to Atlanta from living in San Francisco with my older sister.

During the latter years at the university, I began to explore the possibility of moving up the academic ladder to become an academic dean. I applied to three or four colleges, hoping to secure a position at a state college or university. I am convinced now that the failure to achieve this had to do with my being unmarried. My resume was impressive, and the interviews always went well, so I thought. I am not sure, even now, that had I got a position I would have returned to Atlanta to take care of my mother.

Chapter Eleven
My Faith Looks Up to Thee

My faith looks up to thee… (Eph. 3:17)

Leaving Detroit and a tenured teaching position at the University of Detroit presented many challenges. The vice president and dean at the Interdenominational Theological Center (ITC) had decided to reduce his teaching load at ITC. I had applied to ITC, not knowing this, but knew the Bible facility there was not noted for any specific things. There was not a distinguished member among its staff. With a PhD in biblical studies with emphasis on the Hebrew Bible and a Rockefeller Fellow, I thought my chance at being hired was good. I had previously interviewed at the ITC in 1970, and I believe I applied to each of the Black colleges in Atlanta at the same time I applied to the ITC. I was hired as an associate professor of biblical studies.

At that time, Dr. Shockley was president and Dr. Charles B. Copher was vice president for academic affairs. Dr. Robert Briggs chaired the biblical studies department, of which there was one other faculty member— Prof. Murray Branch. Both Briggs and Branch taught New Testament studies. I discovered an institution that, to me, was overly structured, including the six seminaries' deans who attended faculty meetings. The school (ITC) was more staff focus than student focus. The chairperson of the Finance Committee, Mrs. Elizabeth Littlejohn, and the register, Mrs. Edith Thomas, for the most part ran the institution. This approach was strange to me given that I had come from an institution where student presence was central to the mission of the school. There would be three faculty meetings every month, two of which included the denominational deans. The meetings were scheduled to begin at 9:00 a.m., which rarely happened. Once it did begin, whenever someone arrived late, the previous proceedings were summarized for that individual. The deans' participation was scheduled for a later point in the meeting. When the deans arrived, they were given a summary of the proceedings of the faculty meeting. Often, many of the issues discussed prior to their arrival had to do with students. With this, the deans then could ask and participate in the meeting.

My ten years at the ITC went quickly, but often with distractions. As a department chair and faculty member of the board of trustees, and having served on many committees, sometimes I felt completely overwhelmed. Working as a full-time faculty member trying to get established in Atlanta by buying a home, I took on a part time job at a local Howard Johnson hotel. Since I had experience working in the hotel industry, I became the night auditor for the hotel on Virginia Avenue near the Atlanta airport.

Working weekends at Howard Johnson proved stressful in many ways. The hours were from 11:00 p.m. until 7:00 a.m., ending on Monday morning. I had a few class meetings on Monday morning beginning at 8:00 a.m. The income from Howard Johnson allowed me to move from a rental to a home in the Virginia-Highland area of Atlanta. This was and still is a middle-income area located near several of Atlanta's most upscale communities, including Druid Hills and Buckhead.

Preparation for four classes, meeting and counseling students, faculty meetings, and working weekends led to virtually no social life. Additionally, living with the woman who had moved to Atlanta proved difficult given that I had little energy and time to spend with her. While working weekends, one of the deans, an AME brother, asked me to teach an introductory New Testament course at Morris Brown College, which is adjacent to the ITC. The faculty member who taught this course there had died and the New Testament was a requirement of all students.

Even now, after all these years, I wonder how I was able to manage all of this and not have a nervous breakdown. Much of this was possible because my need for so few hours of sleep. I remember coming home and not remembering when and how I had gotten there. I attribute my ability to the saying, "The Lord watches over old folks and fools." Certainly, this He has done for me over the years, for which I am grateful and thankful.

Chapter Twelve
The Long Journey

"Nobody told me that the road would be easy..."

Even now, after so many decades of obstacles and challenges, I am still amazed at how I had such a good life. Moving back to Atlanta in 1976 meant a great deal in what is now termed "downsizing." My major issue here was income. Let me digress here a bit. For many years, I have been a reader of *Consumer Report*. Before purchasing many things, I research such in *Consumer Report*.

Doing my own laundry has been something I have done all my life. Once reading about detergents, I was led to an Amway product that was its highest rated one at that time. This led me to purchase the product that brought me in touch with an Amway distributor who worked in the Virginia-Highland neighborhood where I lived. Through this, I became a distributor, which was then a part of the pyramid structure (a multi-level structure) of Amway. I needed extra income to simply maintain any reasonable semblance of being a professor. Using the Amway method, I added agents in what is known as a "downline." I had not been a salesperson since my childhood days. What I discovered was that as a teacher and instructor, I had always been a salesperson, selling education rather effectively.

Amway introduced me to the multi-level marketing concept. This allows one to build a business by recruiting others to not only purchase products but to become distributors of those products. Today, this is a widely used method found in operation on social media. There are many positive aspects to this, as well as those that are not so positive. As an Amway distributor, I had to purchase products for orders. I sometimes had closets stacked with detergent, beauty items, and household equipment. Even after many years out of the company, I still own and use an Amway floor sweeper.

A part of being a distributor was attending regular Amway meetings held by my "upline," usually on a Saturday morning. Here, I was taught selling techniques such as a "successful" closing. There was always featured products with their qualities being highlighted to increase sales.

Quarterly, semi-annual, and annual gatherings of distributors allowed me to travel throughout the southeast and to national meetings in places such as Chicago and Las Vegas. My first trip to Las Vegas was to an Amway Convention that had thousands from around the world in attendance. Always, the corporate leaders and very successful distributors would be featured speakers. Workshops on a variety of subjects dominated what would be called "free time." Sunday morning always began with a worship service at the convention center.

It was at a local Amway meeting that I met David Smith, a vice president with A. L. Williams, a Primerica Company. A. L Williams was an insurance and investment company founded by A. L. Williams, a Georgia native. It, too, was a multi-level marketing organization. I do not recall the exact reason, but David asked me about my investment for retirement since I told him that I was a faculty member at the ITC.

Previously, I mentioned that I understood it would be difficult to live on the projected income from TIAA-CREF once I retired at the age of sixty-five. I had begun a separate investment with a company associated with American Express, IDS. My returns had been stable. David asked about my life insurance coverage, given that I was single with no children. This discussion led him to tell me about the basic philosophy of the A. L William Company: "buy term and invest the difference." My life insurance was with the Life of Georgia, as was my mother's.

David Smith asked if he could visit me at my home. During our visit, he shared with me what he did, the types of returns his clients were getting, and his income. He invited me to his office in Decatur, Ga. Here, he presented me with the multi-level marketing approach used by the A. L. William Company. Hearing the investment opportunities, I got an invitation from the faculty of the ITC to allow David to come and make a presentation. In the meantime, I had signed up to be an agent.

A number of faculty members became my clients, and I began to build an organization that would lead me, in a very short time, to being a regional vice president with the company. I was able to recruit some faculty members and denomination deans as clients and was able to recruit one dean into the business.

Previously, I mentioned my interest in finances and my enrollment in an MBA program in accounting at the University of Detroit where I taught. For some reason, once back in Atlanta, I applied for the MBA program at Georgia State University. Georgia State required that I take the GMAT exam. I had not taken such an exam since applying to the School of Theology at Boston. My thought was that I would not make a high enough grade to enter GSU. To my surprise, I did and was admitted to the MBA program.

This bit of digression allows me to take and address the rapid rise I had as an agent with the A. L. William Company. Insurance and investment agents must pass a serious of exams to be licensed by the state for insurance and to be licensed by the state and federal government to sell investments. The A. L. William Company provided classes in all the areas of its work where licensing was required. Upon completion of the life insurance class, I took the Georgia State exam to become an insurance agent. I scored above 90 out of a possible 100. Doing so made me an agent but also allowed me to begin building my own organizational downline. Within six months with the company, I had achieved the status of regional vice president, with David Smith as my upline, within the Keith Phillips organization, where Keith was the senior regional president.

Once receiving my insurance license, I began the process to acquire the license to sell investment securities. Again, I took a class, following which I took the national investment exam and again passed with a score above 90 out of a possible 100. David Smith was so impressed. He told me he knew of no one in the entire organization who had done so well so quickly. I moved quicky to qualify as a registered twenty-six security representative. This allowed me to market all types of investment securities.

Thus, within a year with A. L. Williams, I had become a regional vice president and a registered security agent. As such, I marketed term life insurance, securities through the First American National Securities and mortgages through the ALW Home Mortgages, Inc. My organization continued to grow, and eventually, I was promoted to a senior regional vice president status. I acquired my own office building in College Park, Ga.

I have taken this long departure because my advancement with A. L Williams, which later became Primerica, affected my ministry. Within the guidelines of Primerica, a rule stated that a vice president had to be a "captive agent" of the company. This meant no outside employment could be pursued. My senior regional president, Keith Phillips, sought to make me relinquish my ministry at the Solid Rock Church. Fortunately, I knew there were others in Primerica who had responsibilities outside of the company, one of whom was Keith Phillips' superior, who pastored a church in Macon, Georgia. Here began an ongoing conflict between the two of us that got to be rather nasty at times.

Keith held weekly Monday morning meetings for his RVPs. Such meetings were held prior to a live stream of a weekly program from the headquarters in Duluth, Georgia. On some occasions, his organization was invited to be a part of the live audience. On many occasions, I drove to the Breckinridge address in Duluth. In my early days as an

RVP, I traveled to the company's various warehouses for supplies and to take securities deposits.

The Primerica officers held frequent emergency sessions. Here, new ideas for marketing and new products were introduced. The company was constantly growing with new products and expanding beyond the States. It was an exciting time for me as a new entrepreneur. I learned much that helped me build and expand the ministry of the church. As mentioned above, I long understood the church as a business where adding "new" ideas and members kept the church relevant.

Back to the emergency meeting concept. On an ongoing, irregular timing, Keith would call an emergency meeting at his home in Lithonia, Georgia for midnight. Reaching his home for me was an hour drive, mostly on I-20 East. Seldom was there any real demonstrated need for such meetings, especially given the weekly updates provided at his Monday sessions in Decatur. I do not recall how long I would make these late-night sessions.

One evening around 2:00 a.m., along I-20 Westbound, I felt extremely drowsy and pulled over to the side of the highway. Almost immediately, a DeKalb County police car pulled up behind me with its blue lights on. A Black female policewoman came to my window and began questioning as to why I was there and did not have my blinker on. It was at this precise moment I decided I would not attend any more of Keith's midnight emergency meeting. This decision increased Keith Phillips' displeasure with me in his organization. He began to bring a series of charges against me with his upline to get me out of the company. None succeeded because each was false and unprovable. One was that I had become an agent of a competing insurance company.

It was not difficult to understand the lack of moral character of Keith Phillips. I had seen his relationship with David Smith decline as David demonstrated more independence. David was his first RVP and top earner. There were calls to my office at various times of the day to see if the office was open full time as required by my contract. There were unscheduled visits by members of Keith's team to see whether I was in the office. There were beeps from Keith's office to see if I had the beeper on. I grew weary of this and decided it was best for me to leave Primerica. Thus, the year I turned sixty-nine, I did so with no regrets. There were those in my organization that asked me to stay and fight Keith, but I simply did not have the energy. Because I choose not to pursue this, Primerica reduced my contract, and I resigned. Eventually, I sold the office building to another Primerica RVP.

Chapter Thirteen
Putting It All Behind and Moving Forward

"He prepared a table before me in the presence of my..." (Ps. 23:5)

As I have stated several times now from that familiar poem: "Life for me hasn't been a crystal stair." The building of a solid foundation for the ministry came from my time learning in seminary, working as a youth minister, building a business, and simply living life itself. I still find the successes I have had odd, knowing where I started in Summerhill and Peoplestown in Atlanta during the days of the Great Depression and World War II.

While I was away in the military, my home church, Solid Rock Missionary Baptist Church, had a new pastor installed, the Rev. L. C. Robison. Under his leadership, the church relocated from Summerhill, off the dead-end, dirt road of Reed Street, to South Atlanta, 747 Martin Avenue, SE. The church acquired the property of Trinity AME Church that had relocated to the west side of the city. For some reason, relocating gave rise to a new name for the congregation: The Greater Solid Rock Baptist Church. The relocating did not change the urban/rural status of the orientation.

As an AME church structure, traditional Baptist items and equipment were lacking. There was no baptismal pool and no kitchen, and the bathrooms were in the basement that was a dirt floor.

As an AME structure, there was an altar rail. The pastor's study shared space with a small bathroom. I believe the relocation took place in 1970. I returned to Atlanta in 1976. A conflict over mismanagement of the church's funds required the church to terminate the pastorate of Rev. Robinson. He had a brother with the same first name, whose family had become members of the church. Deacon Robinson and his family were active in many areas of the life of the church. Today, the men's ministry of the church is named the Lonnie C. Robinson Men's Ministry in honor of Deacon Robinson. His widow is a member of the mothers' ministry, and his daughters and in-laws are active in various areas of the life of the church.

Upon the termination of Reverend Robinson, the church called the Rev. W. O. DeVaughn, who was serving at a small Baptist church east of Atlanta. The church, as like many others, held Sunday worship services on the second and fourth Sundays of each month; the Sunday school met every Sunday. On fifth Sundays, the congregation participated in convention work.

Reverend DeVaughn, a graduate of Morehouse College, was the prototypical Black Baptist preacher—tall, a singer, with a wife and several children. His wife served as the church musician; his daughter sang with the Houston Opera Company. His sermonic presentations were often rousing, with shouting taking place. Reverend DeVaughn moved the church to hold services every Sunday except for the fifth Sunday. He brought in an assistant who conducted worship the other two Sundays of the month while Reverend DeVaughn continued to serve the rural church where he was when Solid Rock called him as pastor. The congregation began to grow a bit under his leadership.

As had been the custom, the congregation allowed the pastor to pay the mortgage note on the church. Eventually, several members of the church came to know that Reverend DeVaughn was not paying the note; he was pocketing the money for his own benefit. With the support of the deacons and mothers of the church, he was terminated. This meant that the church minister of music departed, as well as some members.

Reverend DeVaughn transitioned to an AME church in Decatur, Georgia, and the church then sought an interim pastor.

One day, I had to go to the Rexall Drug Store on Broad Street in downtown Atlanta. When leaving, I noticed Sister Grace Barksdale at the MARTA bus stop. (Previously, I have spoken of her and her daughters, with whom I would go to church when we lived in Peoplestown. In other places, she is referred to as Mother Barksdale or Mother Grace.) I stopped and offered to take her home. Once we reached her home on Primrose Street, she asked me to come inside because she wanted to share something with me. The sharing had to do with the church's termination of Reverend DeVaughn and its wish to not have the youth pastor serve as an interim. She asked me if I would serve. I thought about it, maybe for several days. I was a regular attendee at the church, although I was not there every Sunday.

I finally called Sister Barksdale and gave her my consent to present my name to the congregation with the clear understanding that I had no interest in being the pastor. When the church conference met, the recommendation, I am told, met with unanimous approval. This happened because of my long relationship with the church, even when I was away from the city. Each time I came home, I made it part of my visits to attend Solid Rock. This decision did not sit well with the youth minister, Reverend Broughton. Given that I had agreed only on an interim basis, the church immediately formed a search committee for a full-time pastor. One of the first names it received was that of the youth pastor who remained at Solid Rock.

Given my career at the ITC, I had access to a variety of students and got to know several pastors. Several from this category also submitted their names. One was one of my former students at the University of Detroit. As it turned out, between ten and twelve students at the ITC had been students of mine in Detroit. They were from various denominations.

Having served as a youth minster and interim pastor in the Boston area while a student at Boston University, I came to believe that to survive and thrive as a congregation, The Sold Rock Church had to make som major adjustments, the most basic being to understand the meaning of being a missionary church given that it, at that time, had little mission outreach, and this only through the Mothers' Helping Hand ministry.

When working at Ebenezer in Boston, I had discovered the importance of having the church involved in the life of the community. The Greater Solid Rock Church was not doing this. In this south Atlanta community were several organizations that I came to know. The South Atlanta Civic Association, the South Atlanta Land Trust, and the Carver Homes. In addition, I knew the principal of the nearby high school, Carver High, Dr. Norris Hogan. I first came to know Hogan as a fellow faculty member at Howard High School and a co-director of the Army Education Center in Ulm, Germany, where we both served. Almost immediately, I began to attend meetings of the Atlanta Land Trust, where I became aware of its involvement in attempts to bring business and other activities to what seemed to have been a dying neighborhood. Some members had children who attended Carver, others lived in the nearby public housings, Carver Homes.

Dr. Hogan proved to be a valuable resource, and he invited me to become a member of his advisory committee. At that time, Carver had a day care for the children of its students. This was the only day care in the immediate area. My involvement with the South Atlanta Land Trust got me involved in the work of such an agency. At the time, its director was Craig Taylor. Craig saw my interest in the community and got me involved with the Atlanta chapter of Habitat for Humanity.

The Land Trust recognized the real need for a functional day care facility in the area. One day, Craig Taylor asked if he could arrange to meet with me at the church. At this meeting, he provided the necessary data to show the need for the day care. He told me that the Land Trust could not establish one but could assist in its development and funding. He finally asked if the church would agree to sponsor the day care facility. I took this recommendation to the congregation, which meet with its approval. Given that the area was zone residential, we needed to seek a rezoning status from the City of Atlanta.

Once the zoning petition was completed and filed, the South Atlanta Civic Association came out in strong opposition, including filing for an injunction to keep the project from moving forward. This proved to me something in which the church should not have to spend money to defend. At that time, we were in negotiations to purchase a vacant house just behind the church. The church was located on a corner lot with an adjoining lot on Martin Avenue. We were growing and needed additional parking space and rooms for classes. The intent was to develop the house into a youth center.

Once it was clear our church was facing opposition to its positive movement, the conversation turned to what we should do. Many were moving from South Atlanta; the city of Atlanta was transitioning. Some members suggested that once again we should give serious thought to our future and where that should be. During this time, I suggested that we begin a fundraising process to help in funding our decision. The suggestion was made to encourage each member who could make a monthly investment into a mutual fund. At that time, Pioneer, a mutual investment fund, allowed a minimum monthly investment of $25.00. I said that within the next two to five years, our investment would be significant and put the church in a better position for its future.

At the annual church conference, the issue came up as to where we were with finding a pastor. Sister Barksdale said that the church should ask me. I said that I had made it clear from the outset that I had no interest in being the pastor of any church. Sister Barksdale then pointed out that I had been there for more than a year and mentioned what was happening with the church. I thought for a moment and said yes to the offer. It was at that point that my relationship to Solid Rock changed from just a member to its minister. I chose the term minister over that of pastor given my desire to serve the church and its community. The deacons raised the issue of setting a date for my installation as the minister of the church. I asked what where they going to install me to do that I was not already doing—performing marriages, baptisms, funerals, baby dedications, etc. I told them the money the church would spend for the installation could be better used paying off the mortgage.

The decision to become the minister of Solid Rock probably was one of the most significant ones of my life. It provided me an opportunity to bring together my educational training, my financial services, my multi-level marketing skills, and my desire to always do my best. The workload continued to be overwhelming. I still wonder after all these years how I survived.

Chapter Fourteen
Developing the Church to Move Forward

"I can do all things through Christ who strengthens me..." (Phil. 4:13)

There was much repair work needed for the church. It had been an AME church, which meant there was no baptismal pool. There was no central heating or air conditioning, and the two rest rooms.
were in an unfinished, dirt-floor basement along with a small kitchen area. The walls in the sanctuary needed painting. It was clear that for some time the church building had not been maintained very well. The needs were very real.

I forwent a salary, since working at ITC and with Primerica, I could afford to do this. Not doing so allowed the church to begin some much-needed work at the church.

As with most non-profits, there were annual fundraisers. We were able to retire the mortgage rather quickly. We had specific fundraisers to install a baptismal pool, central heat, and air conditioning.

The walls inside needed painting, and bringing this to the attention of the congregation, I was told the estimates were too high at the time and we should do this later. I said to the church, there is no reason we cannot do that ourselves. We need probably six to eight gallons of paint with rollers and brushes, and volunteers could do this ourselves. One fall, when I was at an annual AAR/SBL meeting in San Francisco, I returned and discovered that the walls had been painted. Inquiring as to how this took place, I was told that Sister Dennie Mae Maxwell (Slocum Barksdale) had contacted four of the organizations of the church with the proposal that each contribute equally to the purchase of the supply and sent someone that week to assist in the painting. They had done an excellent job, to which I said to them, "I told you, we could do it."

At Solid Rock, each auxiliary had its own treasury and each choir had and paid for its own pianist. The task was clear: to move the church toward a centralized financial support system. One of the first steps toward this occurred once Rev. DeVaughn had been terminated. His wife had been the musician for the church in general, which meant she played for the Sunday school and other groups whenever a musician was needed.

There was a clear need for a musician for first Sunday services. Initially, I played the piano that provided the music. I knew that this was something I could not do over the long term. I do not recall specifically when I met Dr. Alvin Simpson, who at the time was the minister of music at Providence Baptist Church, one of the neighboring churches. Through him, I was put in contact with Susie (Sue) C. Hampton, who had a music school in Decatur, Georgia. She offered classes in piano, organ, and drums. It was through her that I contacted the Rev. Ann Smith, who agreed to work with us until we could find a permanent musician.

For me, life has somehow allowed me to encounter the right person at the time. Reverend Smith was the former wife of the Rev. R. Julian Smith, pastor of the Mt. Moriah Institutional Baptist Church near the Morehouse and Clark College campuses. She had been on staff there as well as serving as a musician at Salem Baptist Church on Baker Road in the Dixie Hills area of the city. Both Mt. Moriah and Salem were prominent and growing churches.

With the aid of Rev. Smith, we convinced the three other choirs of the church that she would become the musician/director for the entire church. This further strengthened the movement toward a centralized governance for Solid Rock.

In conversations with Rev. Smith, I learned that her family was originally from Eatonton, Georgia, where my mother's family had lived. It turned out that we were distant cousins. From her, I learned much about the Randall/Andrews families and their lives in Eatonton. At that time, Rev. Smith was conducting worship at her home in the Grove Park area on the west side of the city. She had a son whose life was disorganized and who was a drug user. I got to know the family and the community rather well.

Rev. Smith made it clear that she could not be with us for the long term. I do not recall how I first met Chuck Williams, who was the minister of music at a church in Gainesville, Ga. He was also a mid-level manager with Southern Bell. It may be that I heard his choir performing. Chuck had a degree in piano and was from a family of preachers in the Albany area of Georgia. I decided one Sunday to drive to Gainesville to hear Chuck's choir. At that point, it occurred to me that he would be the ideal musician for Solid Rock. He was at a large Baptist Church with one choir of almost one hundred. Solid Rock was a small church with several choirs, none of which had more than fifteen members, and each with its own musician.

Chuck lived and worked in Atlanta, so he had to drive to Gainesville for rehearsals and worship services. Our budget at that time was around $10,000, with me being non-salaried. I convinced Chuck Williams to give up his position in Gainesville to work with us with the assurance that, as the church and its finances improved, so would his salary. My relationship to the church made me aware of the importance of good music.

Chuck Williams proved to be an exceptional addition to my ministry. We had a strange, spiritual connection to the degree that I could be thinking of something related to my "Spoken Word" and Chuck would have the appropriate music for it. Chuck was also the music director for the entire church. Gone was the individual pianist for each choir and each choir controlling its finances. Chuck had us hire a bass and drummer.

As this was developing, so was my work with Primerica. Becoming a regional vice president meant that I had to have my own office. David Smith had office space in his office on Covington Highway in Decatur. I rented space from him. Above, I mentioned the character of David, which soon led to a fallout and a realization that I would be better off in a different location. Conferring with Keith Phillips, he introduced me to Herb Lewis, a real estate broker/dealer for a Century 21 Real Estate affiliate. Herb was a million dollar seller with his own franchise.

Herb introduced me to an agent, John C. Carmichael, who had an office complex at 3079 Campbell Rd., Suite 201, not far from my home. Herb asked me if my church was interested in relocating to the suburbs, as so many Black churches were doing. I told him that now we were not financially ready to do so. He asked me to at least look at a church that was on the market in Riverdale, Georgia. Although I am a native of Atlanta, I had never heard of Riverdale.

Within a few days, I called the Rev. William Scarborough of the National Heights Baptist Church in Riverdale. I set up an appointment to visit and walk through the facility. It was located on a ten-acre plot on Camp Road. Reverend Scarborough told us there was already a pending contract, but the intended buyer was having trouble securing financing. The Rev. Joseph M. Ripley, pastor/founder of the Body of Christ Church International, USA, had the contract.

I thought the facility was more than what we were looking for or could afford. I had been told the original asking price and who had made the offer. I contacted Pastor Ripley and asked what the offer was. He informed me that it was none of my business and hung up his phone. I told the Solid Rock congregation about all of this. Some asked to be taken out to see the facility. That following Saturday, we meet at the church on Camp Road. National Heights had already built a new facility in Fayetteville. Those who met me at National Heights asked if we could pause to pray after we were done touring the property. I said yes, and we engaged in a "sentence prayer." When this was over, they said we should purchase the property. I said that we should at least look at more before deciding. I was assured this was the decision needed. At the next church council meeting, a resolution was passed unanimously to proceeded in the process of relocating our congregation to Riverdale.

We made an offer to National Heights that was a bit lower than its asking price. That was in April 1986. Our offer was accepted, although we did not have the finances and did not finalize all of this until August of that year. All of this was done on faith, believing indeed that God had not brought us to this point to leave us. We had not sold or rented out our property in South Atlanta. So, at that time, the Solid Rock Church controlled three pieces of real estate: Reed Street in Summer Hill, Martin Avenue in South Atlanta, and 6280 Camp Road in Riverdale.

Our task was finding a lender to complete the purchase. Remember, this move to Riverdale came when we had about fifty active members and a budget of around $10,000. I inquired as to the process of seeking such a loan and was told the need to complete a loan package. I inquired of Herb Lewis what this entailed. He told me there were agencies that did such and, given the asking price for the property, it would run about $30,000.

I inquired as to what constituted a loan package. Having the experience of writing a successful grant proposal for the ITC to fund its Office of Institutional Development, I thought I would undertake the writing of a loan proposal. This required the gathering of much factual data, including the demographic of the neighborhood to which we were interested and the one where we were located and material on the shifting pattern of housing in the metropolitan area, including public school data. When completed, it was professionally typed and put into the appropriate form. The issue then became to whom should it be submitted.

The loan proposal was submitted to several banks in Atlanta. I was informed that the Trust Company of Georgia had a good relationship with Black churches. I made an appointment with them, and they agreed to meet with us and discuss the funding. They had reviewed our proposal and told us that to proceed with it, the church would have to have a board of trustees rather than just a finance committee.

The church agreed to the creation of a board of trustees, which meant we had to amend the by-laws and constitution of the church. We did so by deciding to re-constitute the entire legal documents. Upon my insistence, in most cases, participation in the life of the church was open to anyone. Where there were age requirements for membership on official boards, this was changed. The concept of boards was changed to ministry. Thus, now all the auxiliaries of the church are titled ministries.

The task became that of organizing a trustees' ministry. We accomplished this rather quickly. The bank approved us for 80 percent of the asking price of the property, with an interest rate of 13 percent. National Heights provided a second mortgage, so we were able to secure complete funding for the purchase. The task then became assuring the income of the church would provide us with enough to make each monthly payment.

Once it was certain that we were moving, even without a signed contract, we put the two properties we owned on the market. We sold the Martin Avenue property to the Rev. Watts of the Capitol Avenue Baptist Church and the Reed Street property to Prophet George J Brooks, III, founder of Spiritual Deliverance Temple. Prophet Brooks, now Bishop Brooks of Detroit, and I had met through Alvin Simpson. Prophet Brooks, a multi-talented musician, did not possess the requested down payment, so we accepted his Hammond III organ. National Heights had removed all its musical instruments, but we had an upright piano. Over the long haul, Prophet Brooks ceased making payments, so we foreclosed on him and rented the property to a Pentecostal/Holiness church. It had a very small membership and soon ran into the same issue we had with Prophet Brooks. Upon the recommendation of our finance committee, we simply deeded the property to the church.

While all of this was happening, my business continued to grow. Moving from John Carmichael's second story space, we acquired office space on the first floor of the Campbellton Road building. Soon after the move, our office was vandalized several times. Although we had not paid much attention to it, cars in the parking lot were broken into. Maybe because we were never there after 9:00 a.m. in the morning, it had not happened to any of our vehicles. The parking lot was behind the building, sheltered from the constant traffic on Campbellton Road. The vandalization made me relocate the business to a relatively large office park: Albright Office Park at 3485 N. Dessert Drive, Suite 120 in East Point, Georgia. Here we stayed for several years, renting additional office spaces as the organization produced more regional vice presidents, at one time eighteen of them. This growth was responsible for my promotion to senior regional vice president. At the suggestion of one of the RVPs, I began to give serious thought to purchasing a building, which would provide much for us.

Once again, Herb Lewis was helpful in pointing out a building he had on the market at 5480 Old National Highway in College Park, Ga. This location was within a five- to ten-minute drive to the church location in Riverdale. For me, these were very good times.

There was continued growth of our congregation based on a plan to visit each neighborhood within a mile radius of the church. Each Saturday morning, a group of us would meet at the church, decide where we would go, and in doing so, stop at every house in the community. Our visit would terminate around noon so that we could re-group at the church by 1:00 p.m. We had a door package to leave with someone at the home or on the door. It contained simple information about the church, including our location and that we were new to the community with a variety of church programs for all ages. Upon my instance the statement was included that anyone could participate in our programs without becoming a member of the church. This statement had a tremendous positive effect on who came, including a group of young boys that used our playing field for baseball practice.

I went each time with a group, always in casual dress. On several occasions, some of the boys would come to the church and ask if they could use the restroom and water fountain. Once, I told them that on a variety of Wednesdays following our Bible study, we served dinner, and they were welcome to come. Eventually, a few of them came to Bible study and Sunday worship, several eventually joining our church. Our youth department grew significantly.

Back to getting a loan approval to purchase the property. Since I had been told that the Trust Company of Georgia had a good relationship with Black churches, I made an appointment to meet with a loan offer and to present our loan proposal. After reviewing it, I was asked if we had trustees. At that time, we did not. The business activities were handled through our finance committee. The loan offer said although the proposal appeared sound, it could not be considered unless we had a board of trustees. This was taken by me as a positive. So, the task became to get the church to approve the formation of a board of trustees. The standards had to be determined for such a board at a Baptist church.

The trustee's ministry was established. Given that this was a new ministry, I insisted that it would have at least one teenager as a member. With this concession, the church moved to rethink its position on the age of members of the deacons and mothers' ministries. Cassandra Morris was elected to the trustees at age sixteen; she also coordinated the weekly Sunday Black History Moment. Earnestine Holloman was placed on the mothers' ministry and Harvey Riggins, Jr. on the deacons' ministry; each was under the age of thirty at the time of their placement.

As a new church in the Riverdale area with two mortgage payments due each month, real urgency had to be given to finances. I learned soon from this experience that a primary task of the senior minister is to stabilize the membership and finances of the church. The congregation approved including in the legal documents the required financial contribution to maintain membership and the church's movement to a tithing concept. We combined the traditional women's and men's days into Unity Day, stressing the need for a unified effort at financing rather than a competitive approach. The decision was made to have two annual, all-church, major fundraisers: Unity Day and the church anniversary. These changes resulted in significant improvements in our fund raising. Herb Lewis sponsored a weekly Sunday morning board cast for us for almost two years. From this, we began to receive contributions from listeners who appreciated our approach, which stressed the music of the church over the traditional preaching of the typical Black Baptist preacher who tended to whoop.

Chapter Fifteen
Everything Is Subject to Change Except...

With a growing membership, many changes began to take place at Solid Rock The fourth Sunday, Youth Sunday, saw an increase in the number of children participating, including a young man from the neighborhood who became the drummer for the Youth Choral. The annual Youth Day saw participation of the youth at all levels of the worship, including providing the Sunday "Spoken Word." A youth band was organized, given the number of young people in the church who played in their school's band and/or orchestra. We were becoming more youth and young adult orientated. I remember one Sunday following the invitation to discipleship that a young boy came forward to join the church. When I asked him why he wanted to be a member, he said because there was discipline and order here. This was one of the primary reasons that we attracted several members from the arm forces stationed at Ft. McPherson and from the local police departments.

The mortgages required a rethinking of the priorities of the church. The bank had financed only 80 percent of the asking price; National Heights provided the second mortgage. At that time, interest rates were high—the bank was 13 percent, National Height's much less. It wanted simply to be rid of the property. Knowing the need for fellowship, I sought a meeting with the three Baptist Conventions: the General Baptists (National Baptist USA, Inc., NBC, USA.); the New Era Baptist Convention (Progressive National Baptist Convention, PNBC), and the Georgia Baptist Convention (Southern Baptist Convention, SBC). I spoke with representatives of the NBC and PNBC and met with the Rev. Dr. Emmanuel McCall of the SBC at his office in Atlanta. Although the church historically had a connection with the General Baptist Convention of Georgia, I never received a call back.

Thinking about the church and its congregation and community, the feeling at the time was that we were not quite prepared to be members of the Southern Baptist Convention. Thus came our establishment and membership with the New Era Missionary Baptist Convention of Georgia, Inc. As a faculty member of the ITC, I had come to know several local pastors whose churches held membership in New Era. At that time, the Rev. Dr. Melvin Watson was president of the state convention and a professor of philosophy at Morehouse College. The Rev. Dr. Charles Sargent, vice president of administration at the ITC, was vice president. Through Dr. Sargent, I was put in touch with Mrs. Esther Smith, a member of Liberty Baptist Church where Dr. Watson was senior pastor. Esther Smith was director of missions for the state convention and the PNBC.

With our membership in New Era, various activities were opened to us. Sister Barbara Morris became very active in the youth department and eventually its director. Our men's ministry became active with the laymen's department and went on a regularly basis to help maintain and care for the convention center.

Let me interject again. As our congregation grew, we developed sixteen ministries for the church, each with its own officers. Each ministry was required to participate in an outreach program. Our Unity Choir went on a quarterly basis to serve early Sunday morning breakfast to the homeless at the Open Door Community on Ponce DeLeon in Northeast Atlanta. The men's ministry went quarterly to work with the Atlanta Food Bank in Northwest Atlanta; the trustees ministry worked with a homeless shelter for women and children in Clayton County. Each of these ministries had to give a quarterly report at our church council that met monthly. During that time, my involvement led to my being the director of the Budget Committee for New Era.

Working with the budget committee, I was engaged with managing the investment funds for the convention as well as searching for property to hold our Youth Department Annual Congress of Christian Education. The Congress was meeting annually at a local church when it became difficult for an individual church to host with classroom space. Each church was required to locate housing for its delegates to the Congress. Eventually, with the recommendation of the Rev. Davie of the GBC, we began to meet at the Georgia Baptist Convention Center in Toccoa, Georgia. Annually, the Convention spent more than $60,000; this covered room and board plus almost endless classroom space.

At the annual convention, questions began to be raised about the $60,000–$70,000 for the week we spent at Toccoa. Over several years, the Conference Center was expanding with a variety of building projects, including a hotel and new chapel. The decision was reached to begin to seek out a place that we owned and could control expenses. One of the member pastors and former president of the Convention remembered that a piece of property in Griffin, Ga., was on the market and could easily fit our desire. The facility, Mr. T's, was a ninety-acre facility with a lake, dormitory, a large meeting facility with a commercial kitchen, and several barns.

Under the leadership of President Harold Baker, we made an offer to purchase the property. The offer to the owner, Mr. Talmage, was accepted. The Convention had, in its own investments, sufficient funds for a down payment. It sought and received a mortgage for an 80 percent loan from a bank in Macon, Ga. President Baker asked me to lead the task force for financing and to develop a committee to oversee the property.

With President Baker's authorization, a Council of Overseers was formed with me as its first director. The initial Council of Overseers had representation from across the state. The members were: The Rev. Dr. D. Earl Bryant, Sr. (Friendship Baptist Church, College Park); Mrs. Margie Burton (Thankful Baptist Church, Augusta); Mrs. Joyce W Davis (Second Ebenezer Baptist Church, Savannah); Mrs. Veronis Hall (First African Baptist Church, Columbus); Deacon James D. Hightower

(Friendship Baptist Church, College Park); Deacon William McCauley (Augusta); The Rev. James Miller (Holy Grove, Griffin); The Rev. Douglas Stowers (Mt. Calvary Baptist Church, Atlanta); Deacon Ralph Troutman (Tremont Baptist Church, Macon); Mrs. Carolyn Trimble (Second Ebenezer Baptist, Savannah); and Mrs. Tempy Walker (West Hunter Street Baptist, Atlanta).

Having worked with several nonprofits, it was clear that there were some legal documents to be developed. A committee was formed to develop the constitution and bylaws, and we hired a person to manage the center—Ms. Vickie Pye, whose family was most active in the life of the community. We filed to incorporate with the State of Georgia and with the federal government to become a 501(c)(3) entity.

Given that the purchased property had been used by many for retreats, conferences, etc., the council put together a plan to market the center to its members and others. Ms. Pye was most instrumental in this. We began an Annual Center Night each July held at the Tremont Church in Macon. Tremont was where the convention first met and organized as a state convention. Each membership church was assessed $1,000, with the clear understanding that at the appropriate time, the pastor of the church would bring forth the check and announce the name of the church and the amount of the contribution. This procedure, modeled after that of the Annual Mission Night, kept the center's budget in balance. The idea to have the pastor bring down the contribution and announce it came from my visitation to several Church of God in Christ (COGIC) churches.

Soon, in addition to membership churches using the facility, other churches and agencies began to do so, too. With the receipt of the some $60,000–$70,000 annually we spent at Taccoa, and the annual contributions for membership churches, it was clear that our plan was working.

After a year or so, a ten-acre adjoining piece of land was placed on the market. The Council decided to purchase this. I do not recall the exact price; we inquired and secured a loan from a local BB&T Bank in

Macon. The front entrance to this track was a small track of land owned by the Norfolk Railroad. With the assistance of one of its employees, we were able to meet with a local representative who agreed to lease us the property at no cost with the understanding that it could not be developed, but we could have a road developed that passed over it that gave us a second entranceway to our now more than 100-acre lot.

Chapter Sixteen
Precious Memories How They...

I have been working on this memoir for some time and just never worked consistently enough to complete it. Now, my realization is that much of my memories as they occurred in time and place are not here. My intent is to complete this manuscript in some form while I am still mentally capable of doing so.

From this point on, I will make no attempt to keep things in any chronological order. What comes to mind that has had a significant impact on my life will be mentioned. I have tried to be somewhat detailed, but age is taking its toll.

Work with the church and various nonprofit organizations opened doors for me to travel and broaden my understating of Christian ministry. The incorporation of youth in virtually all the aspects of the life of the Solid Rock Church was influenced mostly by what I saw happening in a former student's church in Lansing, Mich. Oliver White, whom I probably identified above, made it a point to emphasize his "Children's Moment" each Sunday. I had not experienced this approach before. There were youth Sundays, but these occurred, at best, once per month, usually with the youth minister presiding and providing the sermon. Rev. White emphasized Black history each Sunday with a Black history quiz and an essay in the bulletin related to Black history.

Children's moments and Black history became a part of the Sunday worship at Solid Rock. In addition, the Scripture reading was done by a youth of the church and a youth was appointed to the trustee's ministry. With all this taking place, the youth component of the church continued to grow. There was growth in the Sunday school and in the music ministry beyond the Sun Bean choir.

Note, I grew up in the church, but all these things I witnessed at a community church were new to me and helped me establish a viable youth program at Solid Rock.

My involvement with the South Atlanta Land Trust and Craig Taylor did not end when Solid Rock moved to Riverdale. This work led me to be involved with the local Habitat for Humanity, where I became the treasurer and was involved directly in the planning and construction of several housing projects, one where both former President and Roslyn Carter were actively engaged. We had a daily greeting with the Carters and a dinner at the home of the then president of the Atlanta Habitat for Humanity, who was also president of a local bank.

There is so much for which I am thankful that came from having served on the Habitat Board. I learned that numerous large financial supporters insisted on remaining anonymous. I was surprised at one major contribution from Genuine Parts. I mentioned above the involvement of the president of a local bank. It was this bank where I went when we decided to purchase the property in Riverdale. The gentlemen told me what the bank did with furniture when it renovated. I furnished several offices, including my own, with such surplus.

Also involved on the board was a member of the Day's Inn family, who owned property in Riverdale near the church. This connection proved valuable when the city of Riverdale decided that our church building was not up to code, although it had been there for decades. I knew exactly what was going on, as a Day's Inn heir told me how to move forward.

The Greater Solid Rock acquired the property that had been National Heights Baptist Church, which relocated to Coweta County, south of the Riverdale location. This was done as the Riverdale area was transitioning to mostly Black people. National Heights had a Montessori program supported by students from the Riverdale community. When it relocated, it transferred this program to the New Life Presbyterian Church located nearby on Old National Highway. At that time, New Life had a white minister. Although National Heights had rented its property to a Black church group, it did not allow the Montessori school to remain at that site.

I relate this and should state that National Heights' membership included several local Clayton County political leaders. One of the reasons for locating Solid Rock in Riverdale was due to our desire to provide a day care program in South Atlanta, to which the South Atlanta Neighborhood Association had challenged and took the matter of a zoning issue to the City Council of Atlanta. Within the first year at the Riverdale site, we decided to start our own school, The Solid Rock Academy, and employed Gloria Montgomery as its administrator. It took little time to know she was not the right person for this position. I do not remember all the details now, but Judith Lyons came to see me. She had been operating a small school that had outgrown its location. She discussed merging her program with our new school.

One early morning, I received a call from Mrs. Lyons stating that an officer from the Georgia Department of Education had been there. He declared the building was not for a school and the school had to be closed immediately. I told her I would take care of the matter. I called the office of the superintendent and asked for an immediate appointment, giving the reasons why. I was told such was not possible. So, the next morning at 8 a.m., I was at his office and stated to his secretary that I would be there until I could meet with him. Within an hour, he arrived. Eventually, I met with him and explained why I was there and that there had been a school at that location for some time with no problem. To me, it was a racial issue. National Heights had several politicians in its membership. There were structural issues that should have been corrected while construction was underway. My point was well taken, and the Solid Rock Academy was allowed to remain open and functional.

Several women involved with Habitat were also involved in a prison ministry for women. They informed me that many of their clients were Black but there were no Black volunteers with the program. I was asked to come to one of its meetings. From that meeting, I became actively involved and got several women from Solid Rock to participate. Among these were Barbara Morris and Lili Ingram.

One evening, I was at the Atlanta Airport and met one of my former colleagues from the University of Detroit, Dr. Barbara Carter, professor of sociology at Spelman College, later its provost. I mentioned to her what I was doing with prison ministry for women. She expressed an interest, so I invited her to our next meeting. Dr. Carter became quite involved, eventually becoming president of the agency. It was under Dr. Carter's leadership that we expanded the relationship with women and began a program to house them and their children once they were released. Prison Ministry with Women had an ongoing training program for women while they were incarcerated. Working with Habitat for Humanity, some of the women were receiving training in house building.

Eventually, the Prison Ministry with Women owned two large homes where released women could stay with their children. These women were required to work and/or completed their GED if they did not have one. They understood that their housing arrangement was a transitional one.

Working with several social justice agencies, I got an invitation to meet with the Federal Reserve Board in Boston. This was a time when the federal government was making known its interest in public housing and related issues. This was a three-day conference. Here, I learned there were financial resources and programs available to agencies. Eventually, the Solid Rock Church applied and received several grants from the government.

With a computer lab and willing volunteers from the church, we began a program in computer literacy for all those interested. A committee was formed for the exclusive purpose of developing grant proposals. As indicated above, this is a skill I developed and utilized at the ITC and the SBL.

One of the reasons for the successful development of The Greater Solid Rock Church had to do with its governance policy (polity). The church council was mandated by the constitution of the church to oversee the operation and functions of the church. To do this, there was an annual leadership retreat. This was always held some distance from the church at a conference center, camp site, or hotel with conference rooms.

We met at the Georgia Baptist Conference Center, Toccoa, Lake Arrowhead, Warm Springs, Red Top Mountain, and similar places each year. A committee planned and scheduled the conferences. At each conference, the agenda included a review of the last year's goals and the planning for the coming year and two successive years. At the conference, the leaders would be formed into three separate groups, selected at random. This process made it possible for people to work with those who were not necessarily a member of their ministry.

The task of each group was review and planning. Each was tasked with providing at least five recommendations for the coming year. By the end of the conference, the council had five specific recommendations to make to the congregation at its annual meeting. At times, the process could be frustrating, given human behavior and the tendency to want things to go only one way. The result, at least for the conference, was an agreement for all to work for the common good of The Greater Solid Rock Church family.

Chapter Seventeen
Living in Appreciation...

"Lord, I look back and wonder..."
(Berlinda White, A Heaven in the Ghetto *, 2006).*

I have lost so many memories over the years that God has allowed me to live and prosper in so many ways. This reference is not to finances as to the almost countless resources that have come my way. Today, the term "diversity" is so common. This was not so for almost all my life. So often, as a Black person, I was an "exception."

There is so much to appreciate from all my life. I received many promotions and awards from Primerica, including achieving the status of a senior regional vice president in less than two years and owning an office building on Old National Highway in College Park. Most of this had to do with the ability to connect with people and assist them in their financial needs. From this came lifelong friendships.

From a young age, I had an interest in writing. Working with my high school newspaper, I discovered that I could say things in such a way that made sense to so many. In college, with all that I did as a chemistry major, I had time to be on the school newspaper staff. At commencement, I received an award for my contribution. I had become one of those "investigative" reporters who raise issues about almost anything that had to do with student life. It was at Fisk that I had my first article published in a national publication. Over the decades, I wrote for a variety of publications, from major chapters in academic works, articles in local newspapers in Detroit, and as a featured writer for *Works: Journal of the Church and the World*. I was listed on the cover of the quarterly publication, *The Focus*, fall 2006, a quarterly publication of the School of Theology at Boston University. They did a feature article on my work as minister and educator.

As a pastor and a member of both the Progressive National Baptist Convention and the Southern Baptist Convention, I attended most of the annual meetings of both conventions. One year, when the Progressives were meeting in Detroit, its instructor in Old Testament studies took ill and could not be there. The illness was sudden and took place just as the convention was about to begin. One prominent Baptist pastor, when speaking with the president of the Congress of Christian Education, referred Dr. E. Dewey Smith to me as a highly respected professor of the Hebrew Bible and a pastor who was at the convention. Thus, with this, I became a member of the faculty of the Congress of Christian Education of the PNBC.

Attending some of the many gatherings of the Southern Baptist Convention, Georgia Baptists, and attending sessions of the Black Leadership Retreats of the Southern Baptist Convention, again an opportunity arose to teach a class in introduction to the Old Testament at one of its sessions. Given the Southern Baptist movement toward inclusiveness, I was invited to write for its Sunday school publishing board. To do this, I was invited to a writers' conference at their headquarters in Nashville.

Out of this came my contribution to *Life and Work Pursuits: Bible Studies for Adults*, published by LifeWay Christian Resources of the Southern Baptist Convention.

Above, I referenced membership in the Society of Biblical Literature (SBL) and the formation of Consultation of Black Biblical Scholars. This group now has a permanent role in the SBL. In the late 1980s, Dr. Patrick Henry invited the consultation to hold an initial meeting at the Institute for Ecumenical Cultural Research, St. John's University, Minn., where he was executive director.

The meeting of the Black Biblical Scholars at St. John's University led the group to give thought to a publication of *Stoney the Road We Trod: African American Biblical Interpretation*, with the initial publication by Fortress Press in 1991. The book is still being published and used in a variety of programs at colleges, universities, and seminaries across the globe. The eleven contributors, including myself, agreed that any profits from the publication would be given to The Fund for Theological Education, now The Forum for Theological Education. Yearly, there is an accounting for the residuals.

I found it interesting that my speaking ability got me numerous engagements. Early in the 1990s, I was invited to give the Martin Luther King, Jr. address by the Church Council of St. Paul, Minn. I am positive that this invitation came from my association with Oliver White, of whom I have referenced before. While there, an opportunity was provided to preach at a Sunday morning worship at a local Baptist Church. The New Era Missionary Baptist Convention of Georgia invited me to give the opening message at one of its annual meetings held at Ebenezer Baptist Church, Atlanta.

Serving as senior minister of The Solid Rock Church and being rather active in the community brought opportunities to preach at pastors' and churches' anniversaries, such as New Calvary Baptist Church, Atlanta; West Oakland Baptist Church, Atlanta; and a United Church of Christ in St. Paul, Minn. I preached ordination messages for deacons and ministers. Among these were Ebenezer Baptist Church, Atlanta; Ebenezer Baptist Church, Boston; New Calvary Baptist Church, Atlanta; West Oakland Baptist Church, Atlanta; and several others.

There were a few times when I filled in providing the eulogy for a relative of one of the members of the church. Each of these occurred at the funeral home for a variety of reasons, most often because the person scheduled to give the eulogy did not come. Perhaps the most interesting of these was a service being held for the son of one of the mothers of the church. I did not know the son, but I knew he had many issues, including the use of dope. He was a Rastafarian, and the service was designed as such. The mother had asked me to give remarks. After about a thirty-minute wait for the Rastafarian priest to arrive, the director of Dawsons Funeral Home asked me to take charge, given they had another service scheduled after this one, and there was only one chapel and several viewing rooms. The service proceeded as outlined with piped in music, and as I was finishing the eulogy, the priest arrived. I introduced him and asked if he wished to give remarks. He spoke about the young man and told us he had taken the bus to the funeral home and that was why he was late.

The Solid Rock Church began its own prison ministry with a focus on men. There are probably several reasons for doing so, including getting to know what some other churches were doing. Our church advertised weekly in the Atlanta Journal-Constitution. We received letters and phone calls from inmates across the state. Most of the communication was handled by the deacon's ministry. There were three men with whom I took a personal interest. Of the three, all relatively young, one was a member of Solid Rock. Each was imprisoned for a different offense: Chris, murder; Charles, robbery; and Kenneth, rape. Our member, who had been dishonorably discharged from the Navy, was convicted of armed robbery in Maryland. Of the three, he was the only one with whom I did not visit. Each received letters and money from me on an ongoing basis. Two received early release for good behavior. The third, convicted of rape, spent more than thirty-two years in prison here in Georgia. He was transferred from one state prison to the next. I visited him as far away as Waycross, Ga., and facility in North Georgia near the Tennessee border. He had been convicted in Florida for rape. Georgia had the three-strike law, which meant, for Kenneth, a life sentence with the possibility of parole. Every three or four years, he went before the Georgia Board of Pardons and Paroles. Here in Georgia, after seven years, there is the possibility of parole.

Even with his conviction in Florida and a variety of evidence at a trial in Macon, Ga., he insisted that he was innocent. It turned out that he is a belligerent person who has trouble listening to others. Personally, I engaged an attorney to investigate the issue. Since the attorney would not travel to Macon, Kenneth refused to cooperate with him. He told Kenneth that much of what he needed to know from him could be discussed over the telephone. Each time Kenneth had a hearing before the parole board, he insisted on arguing his innocence. I kept telling him, the hearing was not a trial—he had already had that. He showed no remorse for his behavior. Thus, from the age of nineteen, he was imprisoned here in the state of Georgia for thirty-two years.

Kenneth received parole in late 2021 to a half-way house in Milledgeville, Ga. The parole came due to his increasingly serious medical conditions, including prostate cancer.

Even after all his years of incarceration and health issues, after being released, he is still seeking an attorney to prove his innocence and overturn the conviction—even when the DNA evidence examined by an innocence project years later concluded he had committed the rape in Macon.

I have so many memories. In February 2005, I officially retired from The Greater Solid Rock Baptist Church. There was a month-long celebration with a culminating banquet held at the Atlanta Civic Center. It was well planned and attended. The featured speaker was Dr. John T. Greene, professor of Ancient Near Eastern Studies at Michigan State University. Among the many others were Bishop Donald Battle (Divine Faith Ministries International); Bishop Marvin Thomas (CME Church); President Robert Crummie (Carver Bible College); the Rev. Anthony Bennett (Mt. Avery Baptist Church, Bridgeport, Conn., and former youth minister for Solid Rock); and officials from religious and civic organizations from around the country.

I received numerous letters and emails sent in recognition of the retirement. The office of the governor of Georgia sent a letter. Written, framed proclamations came from Katy Cox, secretary of state of Georgia, and Edwin Bell, chairman of the Clayton County Commission. Later recognition came from Clayton County Black Ministers Fellowship, Dr. Walter Burns, president; the 16th Annual Salute to Black Fathers; and The Concerned Black Clergy of Metro-Atlanta, Inc., Rev. Timothy McDonald III, president, the Rev. Darrell D. Elligan, chairperson. Also, I received recognition from the 2020 Green Light Recipient; "A Shining Star"; the 16th Annual Scholarship Prayer Breakfast; and H. M. Turner National Alumni Association, Inc.

The end of my tenure as senior minister of The Greater Solid Rock Baptist Church was August 30, 2005, at which time the church called as its pastor the Rev. Will Hayes. As of the 1st of September 2005, the ITC had asked me to coordinate their Old Testament Distant Learning program. There were three centers: Miami, Fla., the Washington, D.C./Baltimore area, and New England. I was asked by the academic dean to conduct a semester of Saturday morning sessions from 9:00 a.m. to 12:30 p.m. This provided me with an introduction to the use of modern technology in seminary education. There were about seventy students on site and as many more viewing from the three indicated locations. They could view what was taking place at the ITC here in Atlanta and communicate with me in an interactive format.

In the spring of 2007, I received a call from Dr. Charles N. Hawk, chairman of the deacon board at Friendship Baptist Church, Atlanta, Ga. The call, in many ways, was a surprise. He told me that their pastor, the Rev. William Guy, had announced his retirement and that the church had established a Search Committee to find an interim pastor. Rev. Guy had announced that he would retire at the end of August. Dr. Hawk told me that the church was inviting three people for the position, including the Rev. Joe Roberts of the Historic Ebenezer Baptist Church of Atlanta. I thought to myself, why would they interview two others when Joe Roberts had indicated interest. I went for the interview, and to my surprise, I received a call from Dr. Hawk telling me I had been chosen and asked if I could begin in August 2007 to serve as Friendship's interim.

In April 1862, when the number of Black members had grown to a significant number at the First Baptist Church of Atlanta, First Baptist purchased a small plot of land and gave it to the Black members. This dates Friendship's founding to before the Civil War was over. Both Spelman and Morehouse Colleges began their presence in Atlanta at Friendship Baptist Church. Friendship is the oldest Black Baptist Church in the city of Atlanta.

First Baptist of Atlanta was located on Peachtree Street near downtown Atlanta. I do not remember when I began on early Sunday mornings to watch In Touch Ministry hosted by Dr. Charles Stanley, pastor of First Baptist. I found his messages to be inspirational and the music most appropriate. I did notice there were a few Black singers in the large choir and there was an orchestra. Living in the Virginia-Highland area and when not worshiping at Solid Rock, I attended other services and visited First Baptist. I got there shortly after the service had begun. An usher seated me near the front—I was the third person on that row nearest the aisle. At some point, Dr. Stanley said it was prayer time and that we should take the hand of the persons seated next to us. I was seated between two white people who refused to take may hand. I did bow my head and listen to Dr. Stanley's praying. I had been given a guest card and instructed to place it in the offering basket at offering time, which I did. A few weeks later, I received a call from a member of First Baptist. He thanked me for coming and asked if I would be visiting again. I told him no. He asked the reason why. I told him of my experience there as a worshiper. Having lived in several cities and attending integrated churches, I had not thought that in Atlanta, in this mega church with an international audience, I would have encountered the experience I had at First Baptist. In some ways, First Baptist's attitude toward Black inclusion had not changed since the days it gave its Black participants that land that became Friendship Baptist Church of Atlanta.

Friendship has always been the church home of several prominent Black Atlantans, including the first Black mayor of the city whose father once pastored the church. Among the members, there were Henry and Billye Aaron; Ozell Sutton; one of the original Black marines; the sister of a Tuskegee Airman, who asked me to eulogized her brother; the presidents of Spelman and Morehouse colleges; Dr. Ocie Irons of Clark College; Deacon Charlie Carter, former member of a Federal Reserve Bank; and Dr. Asa Yancey, one of the first Black surgeons at Grady Memorial Hospital. I could go on and on about the congregation and who would be present on a typical Sunday morning where worship began at 10 a.m. and had to be concluded no later than 11:30 a.m. Among such as listed were maids, janitors, and truck and school bus drivers.

I asked Dr. Hawk to send me a copy of the church constitution and bylaws. He did this, along with the financial documents of the church. Friendship owned and operated a fifteen-story senior citizen tower; 216 two- and three-bedroom apartments; and additional property with parking all near the church on Mitchell Street at Northside Drive. I discovered that after I accepted the interim appointment, I was chairperson of the Trustee Board in charge of those properties in addition to the church itself. This was somewhat overwhelming to me.

The membership was more than seven hundred, with forty-five deacons. The operational budget for the housing properties was substantial. The Sunday worship began at 10 a.m. and had to be concluded no later than 11:30 p.m. Asking about this unusual time for worship, I was informed that the church rented out its parking spaces for those attending the Sunday football games at the Falcons' Stadium just three blocks away. The parking was secure, and each space was $25. This was a significant amount of the annual budget for the church.

Accepting the position, I decided to use the title minister ad interim, with the focus on minister rather than interim. The task was clear to me: stabilize the membership and finances. For the first month or so, my sermon focus was on stewardship. The emphasis was to give a clear understanding of the basis of stewardship, which is that God owns everything and has entrusted us to be good stewards of the resources He provides. This series was followed by one dealing with tithe and offerings, again focusing on the biblical basis for such.

In some ways, Friendship was a mission outreach church. On a regular basis on Saturday mornings, it would send its buses out to find homeless people and bring them to the church for breakfast and give them food baskets, MARTA transportation cards, etc. It never encouraged them to become members or to come to Sunday worship. While I was at the church, no one ever came for assistance to pay their rent and/or utility bills and did not receive assistance. There was never any attempt to get anyone needing help to join the church.

The first sermon I gave at Friendship was based on an old hymn of the church, the one I used for my trial sermon in 1963, "Time Is Filled with Swift Transitions." Having read the legal documents and the two histories of the church, I knew it was time to bring the church into the twenty-first century. The membership was open to such changes. The first thing we did was to create a mission statement for the church. This seemed so obvious given that the Baptist church is a mission oriented one. Sometimes, listening and reading the news, it seems that too many churches do not know its mission "to be in the world reconciling it to God through Jesus Christ."

The second series of messages had to do with tithes and offering. Stress was placed on understanding that tithe had to do with more than one's money. It must deal with all aspects of life, including the opportunities to introduce others to Jesus. Again, particular emphasis was placed on the appropriate use of the resources God has provided. I wanted each member to understand the need for him/her to give 10 percent of their time in the service of the Lord. This is what I have discovered is most difficult for those in the church to do. It seems most would rather give 10 percent of their money rather than their time.

With a consistent message and encouragement to share their faith with others, the congregation began to stabilize and grow. Each Sunday, Friendship included in its announcement section of its bulletin an indication as to how it was moving toward its proposed annual budget. Shortly after my arrival, the membership noticed a marked increase in weekly contributions. One member who with his brother owned a hardware store decided that the church could use a new piano. He contributed in excess of $150,000 for the purchase of a Yamaha grand piano that was installed and dedicated in memory of his mother.

One of the historical features of the church was its pipe organ, which some suggested was one of the best in the area. The music ministry was under the direction of Dr. Sharon Willis, chair and professor of music at Clark-Atlanta University. Dr. Willis had made a major contribution to the music scene in Atlanta by writing and producing operas. There was an extensive music staff and several choirs, including one that provided music for all the homegoing services at the church.

The music ministry at Friendship has a long and rich history, including having as one of its directors the late Dr. Wendell P. Whalum, noted hymnologist and composer of Negro spirituals, and Roslyn Lewis, national acclaimed handbell choir developer and director. For a long time, the organist and one of the first people at the church each Sunday morning, was Kenneth Wynn. Kenneth's family had owned a gas station on Davis Street, across the street from Friendship.

New members were not only from other Baptist churches but other denominations as well. With emphasis on Christian education, the church school grew as well as the Wednesday Bible study. The church school instructors were instructed to stop closing their doors and leave them open so that guests would feel more welcome to enter. Also, a major posting of the location of the classes was installed inside the entrance of the church on its lower level at the parking lot entrance.

After a national search for a senior pastor, with some 450 applicants from around the globe, the chosen candidate, Dr. Timothy T. Boddie, was to begin his service on the second Sunday of June 2007.

At the conclusion of the worship service and Holy Communion, the church presented me with a large, engraved plaque containing following wording:

The Son of My Father

FRIENDSHIP BAPTIST CHURCH

Atlanta, Georgia

PASTORAL COMMENDATION

Presented to

The Rev. Dr. John W. Waters

Minister ad interim

for

Exemplary Pastoral Service and Leadership

during the Pastoral Transition

of

FRIENDSHIP BAPTIST CHURCH

2007–2008

Marla Coleman-Holloway **Chair, Deacon Board**	**Charlie Moreland** **Chair, Trustee Board**

One of the members of Friendship was Rev. Dr. Bobby Joe Saucer, a former dean of the Morehouse of Religion at the ITC. He served on an advisory committee for the American Baptist Convention and was involved directly with the search process for the Fellowship Missionary Baptist Church (FMBC) of Minneapolis, Minn.

FMBC was involved with its founding pastor, the Rev. Albert Gallmon, Jr., and the IRS. The church severed its relationship with the pastor. Dr. Saucer suggested that the church take some time before calling its next pastor. He told them about me and my work with Friendship, where he and his wife held membership. In mid-March of 2008, I received a call from Deacon Troy Smith, chair of the deacon board and pastoral search committee at Fellowship. He explained to me the call and asked if I was interested in an interim appointment at Fellowship. The offer was very good, so I accepted an invitation to fly to Minneapolis and meet with the search committee. The interviewing process took place over several days, including me preaching twice that Sunday morning at the 8:45 a.m. and 10:45 a.m. services. There were several associate ministers at Fellowship, but they had been excluded from the process for an interim pastor.

Since Fellowship lacked a senior pastor, I was asked if I would come as soon as my time at Friendship was at an end. That would have been the second Sunday of June 2008. I told them I needed some time to put my affairs in order, given I owned my home and did not plan to rent it or sell it because I had no way of knowing how long the interim position would last. I agreed to come on the fourth Sunday of June 2008.

Fellowship had viewing cameras in the vestibule, outside the entrance to the sanctuary, and in the parking lots. Behind the sanctuary was a multi-level building where Sunday classes were held, and office space was leased by the city. From the pastor's office, all these spaces could be viewed. There were meeting and conference rooms. The main building was not complete worship was held in a gym like setting with a portal baptismal pool. To me, there were several unusual features to Fellowship's buildings and worship space. Some of this challenged my upbring in a small Baptist congregation in Atlanta.

Sitting in the pastor's office on my first Sunday at Fellowship, I decided to view the sanctuary. I had been informed that the deacons led devotions and that the ministers and I would enter at the conclusion of their devotional period. What I saw was several people waiting outside the closed sanctuary doors while the deacons conducted the devotional period. The choir and ministers were to enter from side entrances as worshipers came into the sanctuary.

One of the first changes I made as senior minister was to incorporate the deacons' devotions into the regular worship service. The call to worship would be issued by one of the associates, and with this modest change, more people were inside the sanctuary with the deacons. The deacons saw this as a very positive change.

There were many firsts for me at Fellowship. The music ministry was led by Sanford Moore, professor of music at the University of Minnesota. The congregation was multi-racial. There were several musicians who were white and there were a few officers of the various ministries that were also. On the first Sunday of July, it surprised me that at the call for discipleship, an invitation to join the church, a senior white woman came forward with several others.

Mrs. Darlene Bowman joined Fellowship my second Sunday there as the minister ad interim. During the new members orientation, each person had to meet personally with the minister. Meeting with Darlene, I learned that she and her late husband had served as Methodist missionaries in several countries, mostly in Africa. They had a son, who was disabled. Darlene expressed grave concern about him, wondering what would happen to him should she preceded him in death. The last time I heard from her was in 2013, after her son had died.

As a part of expanding the outreach mission of the church, I made an appointment to visit with the principal of the high school that was across the street from the church. I had been informed that the school was in trouble and faced possible closure. Visiting the principal, who had been there for three years, I was informed that I was the first person from the church to visit. We talked for more than an hour. I told her about both our Wednesday noonday and evening Bible study, where each ended with a meal. She was invited to attend and to invite her staff and students to do so as well. The school sponsored both a boy and girl scout unit. She told us about these, and soon some of these young boys and girls came to our evening Bible study that began at 6:00 p.m. and was over by 7:00 p.m.

Leaving Fellowship in 2009, I returned to Atlanta and joined the Friendship Baptist Church of College Park. It changed its name to Friendship Community Church Atlanta. I began to attend the Wednesday noonday Bible Study. At the beginning of this attendance, on average, there would be ten to twelve people in attendance. Given my theological training, often I found it difficult to sit through the presentation and would challenge whoever was presiding on their understanding of the biblical subject. Eventually, Pastor Donald Bryant asked me to take over the noonday Bible Study.

I thought it best to begin the Bible study with the first book of the Bible and work our way through it to the book of Revelation. I explained to those in attendance that we would not study every chapter of a book and not even study all sixty-six books of the Bible.

Emphasis was placed on Genesis, with the explanation that every issue faced in life is addressed in the book of Genesis from creation, crime, parenting, social justice, and injustice. From the first Wednesday forward, the size of the group grew. The diversity was simply awesome, including people from the community and workers who were off for lunch. For the Wednesday evening Bible study, the church served dinner prior to the study. I asked Pastor Bryant if something of this nature could be done at the noonday session. He agreed, and lunch was served following Bible study. This, too, increased attendance. It allowed also for gathering around tables of people who did not know each other, and allowed them to get to know one another. Bible study ended at the end of May and Vacation Bible School began early June. The summer break lasted until the end of August.

The Wednesday gatherings went well. There were handouts that contained specific sections of the study for the day, with particular attention to words with special significance in the text. Often the comment would be made that the Bible study was more like being a student enrolled at a seminary.

One spring day, while discussing the book of Jeremiah, my mind just went blank. Of all the books of the Bible, Jeremiah is my favorite, along with Genesis. We had gotten to Jeremiah 36, the chapter where Jehoiakim burns Jeremiah's scroll. This chapter allows not only for the discussion of how much of the Old Testament has survived, but also the process of canonization. As an aside, I often thought that my doctoral dissertation should have been based on the lamentations of Jeremiah. It was my intention during my teaching career to do a commentary on the book, with particular attention to the lamentation tradition.

My memory lapse came near the end of the session. I remember asking someone to give the closing prayer and going down to the dining room. The next morning, I called Pastor Bryant, telling him what had happened and asking him to release me from the noonday Bible study responsibility. He informed me that for the most part the administrative responsibilities had been entrusted to Pastor Torin T. Daily, who was his announced successor and that I should call him. This I did. Not only did I speak with Pastor Dailey, I sent him a letter asking him to share it with the noonday group. In it, I expressed my appreciations for their attendance and support of the weekly Bible study. I explained that for some health and age issues, I would not be returning to the group as its facilitator.

Almost every Sunday at the 11:15 a.m. worship, I would be asked by someone when would I return to the Wednesday Bible study. It never dawned on me that Pastor Daily had not shared my letter with the group. About a month after my incident, I ventured to the Wednesday noonday Bible study. This was a great and awaking event for me. I believe earlier I indicated never attending the Wednesday evening Bible study, which was conducted by Pastor Dailey.

What I witnessed was, for the most part, a continuation with the previous Sunday morning worship with a few exceptions. There was a call to worship, an extended prayer period, and an offering appeal. Never had I experienced any of this prior to my being assigned the Wednesday noon session of Bible study. There was an extensive use of audio visuals. During one of these, Pastor Dailey left the session.

He returned and said to the group he has received a letter from me resigning from facilitating the noon session. He did not bother to explain why he had waited to this time to read the letter, nor did he ask me for any comments. At the end of the session, as usual, lunch was served. There, several people spoke to me about missing the approach to Bible study they had been experiencing for several years. I was told and could observe that several people from the community who were attending were not there.

I am very much aware of the need for change to keep up with the times. I have learned, also, that all change is not for the better or in the best interest to those upon whom the change is implemented. The Bible study group had become quite accustomed to an interactive approach, which was not Daily's style. He wanted a mid-week worship experience, and that was what he made the noon session into. That was the last time I went to the noon Bible study, given I attended Sunday morning worship.

The caption of this chapter indicates my looking backward and wondering a great deal. As is indicated, so many times, I have traveled and lived in many different and diverse places. None of the places proved to be as challenging as it was to move to Christian City, a bit south of the Atlanta Airport. The move was made necessary because the living conditions at Walden Lakes continued to deteriorate with no assurance that such would cease. I thought when I moved to Walden Lakes that would be the final place for me as I planned and completed my estate plan. It's so true that what appears on the outside is no real indication of what is on the inside.

I carefully packed to move, numbering each box and indicating on the outside its content. I engaged a moving company that I had used only once from a reference of a dear friend. My move was to Christian City, about five miles from Walden Lakes. After starting to unpack, I was looking forward to the process, which I thought would be simple given each box was numbered. To my surprise, about the third day, I discovered that four of my boxes were missing. I called the moving company to speak with the manager. He never returned my call; I reported the theft to the Union City Police Department. They took a report, and after several days, I went to the police station to inquire where the case was going. I was not surprised when I was told that my case was not a priority for the Union City Police Department.

In the stolen boxes were my birth certificate, passport, veteran papers, several old watches, and other pieces of jewelry. There was no need, I decided, to file a claim. I took some time and frustration to just get the paperwork I needed to file for a Veterans Administration ID card. The birth certificate replacement was rather simple.

Later, reading an article in *Consumer Report*, I found out that what had happened with me and the movers is rather common and that most do not file a claim. It stated that when moving, prior to the movers' leaving, you should climb into their vehicle and check to see if they have hidden anything under blankets. So, although I do not plan to move again, I learned something.

As with others, I had several items delivered by Amazon and UPS taken from my front door. But, maybe the most disheartening thing about living at Christian City was my attempt to share in its Wednesday Bible study. The teacher or facilitator would be described as a biblical fundamentalist to a "t". It was evident that she was primarily Pentecostal in terms of denomination. And some of the things she allowed others to claim about the Bible, I had not heard even when growing up in that small, rural, almost totally biblically illiterate church called Solid Rock Missionary Baptist Church in Atlanta. "Lord, I look back and wonder, how I got over…"

With the onset of the COVID-19 pandemic, Bible study was discontinued at both Friendship and Christian City. Once the virus was gotten under control, I thought about going to someone's Bible study. I came to realize that as a professional education with a degree in the Hebrew Bible, it would be most difficult to sit in anyone's Bible study without raising critical questions as to what was being imparted. "How do you teach a people who do not wish to be taught?"

Chapter Eighteen
Look Where He's Brought Me From

Facilitating Friendship's noonday Bible study marked the end of my public speaking career. There were many invitations, but only on rare occasions did I share in the Home Going celebration of someone who was dear to me or a relative.

I began my reflections on my life, paying attention to my place of birth and early home in Summerhill. The above reference to Friendship with so many decades in between now allows me to bring my memoir to some type of end.

The Rev. Donald E. Bryant was responsible for the work at Friendship with the noon Bible study. He also provided several occasions for me to deliver the message at the Sunday morning worship. Having been associated with the church from my early days as a professor at the ITC, I had witnessed the development and growth of the church under Pastor Bryant in so many ways. Over the years, I had begun to encourage Black people in all capacities to put their life story in writing. So, I encouraged Bryant to do the same, especially as he came to a period of retirement.

When Pastor Bryant became senior pastor of Friendship, the church was located in downtown College Park. Under his leadership, the membership began to grow. Even with two services, it was evident that the facility and its surrounding land were insufficient for what was happening at Friendship. Under Dr. Bryant's leadership, Friendship acquired a one-hundred-acre site on the western edge of College Park, now South Fulton, Ga. A main sanctuary building, a gymnasium, an education wing, and tennis courts were built there, all fully paid for upon completion. I said to Dr. Bryant on many occasions that he should put in writing how he was able to grow the congregation and relocate it all debt free.

Pastor Bryant, after his formal retirement, put the Friendship story in writing with the publication of *I Didn't Want to Do It! Memoir of a Sinner Turned Megachurch Builder*, Donald Earl Bryant, DMin. Before completion of the manuscript, Bryant asked me to review an outline of it. This I did, offering some amendments and suggestions. These he accepted and then asked me to write a foreword to it, which I did. The book was published by Guardian Angel Communications Services in 2021.

Mid-morning in late January, early February of 2022, I received a call from Mrs. Jean F. Scott, a very active member of Friendship Baptist Church of Atlanta and the Spelman College Alumina Association. She asked if I had heard that their senior pastor had resigned and suggested I would probably get a call asking me to serve as Friendship's interim minister again. I had heard that all was not going well with a pastor who had been there for almost five years. The following morning, I received a call from Deacon John Blackshear, chair of the Interim Pastor Search Committee. He told me much of what Mrs. Scott had already told me and said that the committee had decided to ask me to return as the church's interim pastor. I told him that I was honored to be considered but had to decline given my age and health condition. As an aside, I told him that I was a bit older than Dr. Guy, for whom I served as minister and interim upon his retirement.

After leaving Fellowship in Minneapolis, several offers came to serve as an interim at both local churches and churches outside of Atlanta. My health would not allow me to consider such offers even remotely, even though I was honored to be considered. All of my life I have had to deal with health issues. This is one of the reasons Henry Waters and I never got along. It is interesting that at an early age, my parents were told my life expectancy was less than five years. Registering for the US draft, I was classified as 1–A. In December 1958, I had major surgery at Hugh Spalding Hospital in Atlanta, that corrected my medical condition. For the past decade or so, I have been under the care of a speech pathologist at Piedmont Hospital, Atlanta, and an audiologist at Northside Hospital, Sandy Springs.

Even though I am no longer active in ministry or financial services, I occasionally hear from those with whom I have been associated. Perhaps the most interesting is hearing from Primerica clients, given I left that company in 2001. I am told that I had given good financial advice and probably could still do so. My response has been, "I have no financial licensing." I have made several referrals and do share with some people how my personal investments are doing.

In March of 2022, I received a call from the chair of the deacon board of Zion Baptist Church, Roswell, Ga. His question had to do with church governance. The church has a relatively new pastor, and some issues were developing. I referred the deacon to contact two Baptist churches in the area that have excellent bylaws and constitutions. I referred him also to some major literary resources on Baptist polity. One of the deacons at Fellowship in Minneapolis asked me to review some of the material that had been submitted by their primary candidate for their senior pastor position.

So, as I approach the ninth decade mark, I can look back and say that my life has not been in vain. A life that began at 2:30 a.m. on February 5, 1936, at what was then the Colored Grady Hospital, located at 17 Butler Street in Atlanta.

I started as senior minister of the Greater Solid Rock Baptist Church, with less than fifty active members and a budget under $10,000, and upon my retirement, the membership was more than six hundred, with an annual budget of almost $600,000. Still, I ponder the call to serve the Friendship Baptist Church of Atlanta with some forty-five deacons, a membership of about seven hundred, and a multi-million-dollar annual budget. From Friendship, with less than a few weeks break, I became an interim at Fellowship Missionary Baptist in Minneapolis, with membership between six and seven thousand, and a multi-million-dollar annual budget. When I arrived at Solid Rock, there was no paid staff, and when I left, there was, as with the case of multiple staff at Friendship and Fellowship.

The committee planning the 94th church anniversary for Greater Solid Rock contacted me and asked if I had a recent publication they could acquire to give as gifts to those attending the annual banquet. I did not, but stated I would compose something that could be used. This turned out to be a series of poetic pieces under the title, *Memories, 94th Church Anniversary, 2017: Pearls of Wisdom, Thoughts & Reflections*. The series contained these pieces: "A Gift of Time," "And So We Celebrate in 2017," "On Memory: A Thing or Two," and "Pastor Emeritus Celebrating the Church Anniversary."

The thought behind "A Gift of Time" is one used by me for many occasions in the lives of many people whose lives have touched me. Let me share at this point the poetic piece as printed in the pamphlet shared at the anniversary banquet.

A Gift of Time

Over the life of each of us, we have received many gifts.

Among these, perhaps the most precious is the gift of memory.

Memory allows for the recapturing of so much. Both the good and the bad are parts of our memories.

It is those precious memories that sustained many of us during trying times.

Times when it seemed that almost all was lost with the exception of hope.

Hope is always future oriented, but should be based on past experiences.

It is the gift of Hope that assures us that life can be better.

Thank you for the gift of thought and time you have given me. Give this very special gift of your time to others.

They too will know your true thoughts and feelings.

Give freely of your time, then others will do the same for you.

Thoughtfulness and generosity require time. Doing so should never be taken for granted.

It is the special gift of time that is becoming rare.

Use the precious gift of time to benefit others.

Recalling and recollecting thoughts is much of what these days are for me. Even after teaching high school in Atlanta back in the late 1950's, I remember certain students, projects, and events as though they were recent. Some of those students made good impressions, while others did not. I remember both types. Clinton Dye went on to be director of the Georgia Department of Children Services. Maybe better recalled are some of those who were students of mine at the various post-high school places where I taught, beginning with the School of Theology at Boston University as an adjunct professor and student in the PhD degree programs.

As a Baptist, there are at least twelve connectional bishops who studied with me. This is no way I can assert that these students reached the bishopric because they were my students. There are AME, CME, UMC, and COGIC bishops who were students of mine. The first is Bishop John Bryant, Jr., AME. The COGIC bishop was not only a student of mine but served as a youth minister at the Greater Solid Rock in

Riverdale. Each of these students took at least one Old Testament class with me, several two or more classes, including Hebrew.

Teaching has always fascinated me. Wherever and whatever I have taught, there have been students whose career paths seemed out of touch with what I was teaching. One of the students in my Old Testament class at Boston was a Maine attorney whose midlife career led him to serve as pastor of a United Method Church in Maine. Above, I have mentioned John T. Greene, the first student whom I taught that earned a PhD degree and retired as professor of Ancient Near Eastern Studies at Michigan State University. George O. McCalep, Jr., had a PhD in physical education prior to enrolling at the Morehouse School of Religion at the ITC. Dr. McCalep developed Greenforest Community Baptist Church into a megachurch with a church school that attracted more than five thousand attendants on a typical Saturday morning. He was a prolific writer, desiring to share with others how he had developed such a successful ministry with community focus and involvement.

I had some ten or so former students who asked me to serve on their Doctor of Ministry degree dissertation committee at United Theological Seminary in Ohio. Among them were Arthur Carson, who became president of the New Era Missionary Baptist Convention of Georgia and Kenneth Samuel, founder of megachurch New Birth Missionary Baptist Church, and later the founder of The Temple, a large UCC congregation in Stone Mountain, Ga.

Two unique requests led me to serve on dissertation defense teams for Alvin Simpson, who received a PhD in psychology from Atlanta University, now Clark-Atlanta University, and Dr. James L. Bumpus, who was the first Black person to receive a DMin degree from Mercer University. Dr. Bumpus served for many years as an associate and youth minister with me at The Greater Solid Rock Baptist Church. Dr. Bumpus was called to the Tremont Street Baptist Church in Macon, Ga., one of the oldest Black congregations in downtown Macon and the home of the founding of the New Era Missionary Baptist Convention of Georgia, Inc.

I have said very little about my health over these decades. Moving to Atlanta, Dr. Charles Harrison, Md., at Piedmont Hospital became my primary physician. He was also the physician for the Atlanta Falcons football team. His schedule and my medical issues led him to refer me to Dr. Phillip Brochmann, also at Piedmont Hospital. Over the years, Dr. Brochmann, who was Jewish, became more than my physician. As medical issues developed, including prostate cancer, he made the arrangement for me to see an oncologist. From a routine examine, he determined that my PSA was getting too high.

As a minister, I got to know both Dr. Harrison and Dr. Brochmann's lives in their religious communities. Dr. Harrison was an active member of Northside United Methodist Church and Dr. Brochmann in the Temple in Atlanta. Dr. Harrison retired from medical practice and is deceased. Dr. Brochmann left Piedmont and became a member of the staff of Kaiser Permanente. He is now retired and moved to upstate New York. Upon his retirement, he sent me a letter announcing that he was leaving and saying how he had come to appreciate our relationship, one that he did not have with any other patient.

I could say many positive things about Dr. Brochmann, including knowing that in many ways because of his attention I have lived more than eight decades. I mentioned the PSA exam that revealed my prostate cancer. Once, I noticed a swelling in my right leg. I went to his office without an appointment. Once his nurse saw it, she said I had a blood clot and needed immediate attention. I was taken by the nurse via an underground tunnel to Piedmont Hospital and admitted. I was hospitalized for almost a week. Each day, on his rounds at the hospital, Dr. Brochmann would stop and spend time with me. Often, this meant praying together. So, it was no major decision to change my medical coverage from Piedmont to Kaiser when Dr. Brochmann moved his practice.

Over the years, many health issues developed, including kidney, gallbladder, vocal cords, and others. Each time, Dr. Brochmann made the referral and checked to see how I was doing. The days of such attention seem to be over. With a number of health issues including psoriasis, diplopia, atherosclerosis of aorta, and other issues, getting help with understanding and treatment became an individual task. Appointments with a medical specialist for the most part became an individual task. With limited skills with IT, I managed to make and keep such appointments, which explain that aging has not prevent me from remaining independent.

Let me go back to the issues of what contributed to most of my achievements. Above, I have referenced Primerica several times. Training and leadership opportunities were there for its members. It was rare that I would miss a session on developing an effective team. At each of the churches where I served, I stressed the importance of being an active member of any committee on which a person was. This supported the primary idea of stabilizing the membership and the budget.

The Solid Rock Church became a Southern Baptist Church and an active member of the Fairburn Baptist Association, a part of the Georgia Baptist Convention. Each summer, the Southern Baptist publishing board, LifeWay, sponsored a Black Church Leadership Conference at one of its major conference centers—Ridgecrest on the East Coast, near Ashville, N.C., and Glorieta toward the West, near Santa Fe, N. Mex.

Each July for almost fifteen years, a group of us from the Solid Rock Church attended the Black Leadership Conference. The expense for such was made a part of the annual church budget. Only those who were sincere in their commitment to the church and its mission were taken. To attend at Ridgecrest, we rented a bus and drove to the conference center; to attend at Glorieta, we flew into Albuquerque and rented a vehicle to drive to the site.

The Leadership Conference provided training in almost every aspect of church life. Early morning worship started each day. To get to it, there was always a long walk. Food was served cafeteria style with many options. Reservations for the conference included several food plans. Our church members got the three meals-a-day plan, even though there were occasions when we went into town and dined. This was especially true in the Santa Fe area. Walking along one street, I saw the Georgia O'Keeffe Museum. I knew her name and work from the museum at Fisk University. O'Keeffe had donated several of her works to Fisk.

Much of the success of my ministry I still attribute to various leadership conferences. Those of the Southern Baptists were most helpful, including those on financial management and developing a wellness ministry. Perhaps the most significant and important one was the introduction to Master Life, a twelve-week program that addressed all aspects of the life of the church: mission outreach, effective prayer ministry, the importance of an effective fellowship ministry, and others.

So, as I stated several times, I have no regrets about my life and the journey it took from the rear of Reed Street in Summerhill to the pinnacle of educational and academic achievement. I do not say this to brag, but to indicate that the place of one's birth does not have to determine the future possibility of achievement. I attribute all of this to the blessings of a God who has loved and kept me despite all that I have gone through.

Moving toward the end, it seems to me that I should take time to call attention to some of the most influential people in my life. I would have to begin this with referring again to my mother, Mary A. Waters, whose gentleness has meant so much to me. My love of flowers came from her—anything growing that has beauty I appreciate because my mother saw beauty in them and shared her thoughts and feelings with me. She should have been a botanist, but such was out of the reach of a colored woman of her time.

Grace Barksdale, whom I referred to earlier as Miss Grace, was entirely responsible for my relationship with the Solid Rock Church beginning in my early childhood. She was responsible for me accepting the position to serve as both an interim and then the senior minister of the church. Miss Grace was what would now be called a female activist. Her involvement in the life of Peoplestown lead to a community health center being located there. One of the ministries of the church, the senior usher ministry, was established in her honor. Her three daughters and most of her grandchildren became members of the church under my tenure.

Thinking backward, there were so many women who made positive impacts on my life. My great aunt, Mary Lue Bryant, who was a businesswoman, taught me how to shop for groceries, as well as the value of always having money on hand. Barbara Lovinggood, a classmate from Turner High School, a majorette, and a French teacher at Howard High School, and Barbara Davis, a graduate of Wayne State with a degree in nursing and a medical degree from Michigan State University are both women whom I dated and each who would have made an excellent wife. I have thought it interesting that both had the first name of Barbara, but each was so different in many ways.

The women in my life have been alike and different in so many ways. There was a time I was sure I would be married by the age of forty. So much happened to circumvent that plan, including my desire to be financially able to support a wife and family. I heard from an early age that most Black men tended to look for wives that reminded them of their mother. No one I dated had fit this description. My interest in the arts attracted me to women who were talented.

Barbara Davis was a model and jazz pianist as well as a registered nurse; Jewelle Anderson, a graduate of New England Conservatory, was an opera singer and a member of Ebenezer Baptist Church of Boston, where I was the youth minister. My last serious relationship was with Dr. Marsha F. Harris, EDU, a native of Bath, S.C., and a member of Tabernacle Baptist Church, Augusta, Ga. I met Dr. Harris at the New Era Congress of Christian Education were we both were on the faculty. I think Dr. Harris' controlling attitude reminded me why a few of my relationships never went that far. I felt the same thing with Jewelle Anderson, whose father had been a physician in Mississippi.

I believe I have acknowledged the influence of several male mentors in my life, noting the positive influence of Dr. John R. Cottin at Fisk University and Dr. Francis Long at Turner High School. I called attention to Herbert Bridgewater, Jr., in both a good and not-so-good influence. I have thought and thought how I first met David Vanderbloemen, a professional painter who worked for Tyler Perry Studios. I engaged David to do some painting at my home on Niskey Lake. He did not have his own transportation, so I would pick him up. We became friends. David played in a minor league soccer team, and I learned about soccer by not only often driving David to matches, but also watching the games. I came to know that David had started college and dropped out with the hope of returning when he could afford to do so. I offered to pay for David to return to school for a semester—paid his tuition, fees, and purchased his books.

I got a call from his school after a month or so asking if I knew why he was not attending classes. I wasted money on what I thought was a way of helping a young man who lived by himself in Atlanta. When I moved from Niskey Lake, I sold David my Jaguar, which was in excellent condition. Where I moved, I had no garage to house it. Within a month, David got drunk and had totaled the car. He had dropped the comprehensive auto insurance on it.

From my life experiences, I now know that the only person whose life you can truly control is your own. Again, I leave no regrets; I learned from the good and bad experiences, some of which were financially expensive lessons.

Before ending "my story," it is appropriate to say something about my immediate family, all of whom are now deceased. In order of their birth, here is who they were and their occupation. All the males were in the military—five in the army, one in the navy, and one (the youngest) in the air force. William worked for C. L. Fain Co. as a driver for the wholesale vegetable company. Ivan aka Alvin were a truck driver and foreman for the Alternman Brothers Grocery Co. Fred retired from the police department of St. Augustine, Fla. A street in that city is named in his honor. Hurbert worked for John Manville's Manufacturing Co. Harry was a butcher. Robert was a machinist and owned his own heating and air conditioning service. Vivian was the owner of a liquor store just outside the navy yard in San Francisco and manager of several parking lots in the area. Mable was a short order cook. Marion died while in the air force. These are the sons and daughters of Henry and Mary Waters. Each lived an independent life.

As I age, I am so appreciative of the members of The Solid Rock Church Family who have keep in touch with me in so many ways. There is no way I could have better friends or support than I get from Robert and Lili Ingram. Robert is a retired army major, and Lili a clinical social worker. I know for each holiday and my birthday they will plan and do something special for me. I also may have mentioned that for my 80th birthday, they planned a banquet in my honor. Many of those who lives had touched mine were invited and attended.

There is a garden at the Solid Rock Church. A couple of the women, Racheal Moorman and Betty Jones Neal, pick and bring me fresh vegetables from that garden. They and others from the church call on a regular basis to check on me and to see if I need something. Because of the grace of God, I am still capable of taking care of myself.

There was a time when I was really and truly independent. As more and more things are conducted using information technology, I found myself often not up to the task of being able to function on my computer and cell phone as I should. Again, people have come into my life who assist me with IT problems. Deacon Marvin Henderson, Sr., from the Solid Rock Church whose career is IT has helped in so many ways. Whenever there is a real complicated problem, I call him. A second person, Louis James Anderson, a real estate project manager, provides similar help. James was most instrumental in me finally navigating the VA system to get an ID card, although I was honorably discharged from the Army in 1963.

As a Black Baptist, I have found myself telling others that I am not a Pauline Christian, considering what he had to say about slaves and people who should submit to others. So, it may seem a bit out of order that here I will insert one of his prayers of benediction.

"Now to him who is able to do immeasurably more than all we ask or imagine, according to his power that is at work within us, to him be glory in the church and in Christ Jesus throughout generations, for ever and ever! Amen" (Eph. 3:20–21).

So, the sickly child from the ghetto has lived that of which Paul speaks to the fullest and then some.

Let me try to bring this to somewhat a close by citing a few lines from the *Pearls of Wisdom: Thoughts and Reflections*:

For every ending, there is also a beginning:

Sounds simple, yet it can be complicated.

We come to the end of a season and begin

another one. Koheleth suggests that there are

27 seasons of life. For everything there is a

time and there is a season....

Printed in the USA
CPSIA information can be obtained
at www.ICGtesting.com
LVHW011032120624
782914LV00016B/622